Christine Lee provides an extraordinary journey of perseverance and persistence! I wholeheartedly endorse this terrific read!

George Fisher
Hall of Fame

It is with great pleasure that I provide this letter of endorsement for *My Hero*. Once you read and comprehend the information in this book you will see how powerful intuition is in our lives. The inspirational information in this book is quite insightful. *My Hero* for me reviews and reinforces the importance of a strong mother in the family, especially when there is no father around. This book also provides clarity of the of the importance of religion in one's life and the life of the family. It is clear that religious principles and practices do provide a positive impact in our lives. Finally, this book helps us to discover who we are and what we can become.

Dr. Warren Washington
Higher Education Consultant

"The oxygen tube was in her mouth, but the Bible was in her hand." Because she knew that true life does not come from oxygen, but from eternal life. *My Hero* provides my intuition, inspiration, and inculcation of life in my soul.

Rev. & Dr. Steve Hong
Senior Pastor of Multiethnic Down Church

My Hero is a story of self-love taught by a loving mother who wanted only the best for her child. Christine delves deep into what we take for granted. Rare is the child that can see the sacrifice a mother will make for her children. And as an adult build a life on that love and strength.

Angela Welch
Bestselling author of *When The Angels Take Me*

Christine Lee is masterful storyteller with vivid descriptions and an engaging narrative. She brings to life her mother's history and her love for her mother is imprinted on every page of the book.

Peggy McColl
New York Times **bestselling author**

MY HERO

A LOVE LETTER TO MY MOTHER

BY

CHRISTINE LEE

 Hasmark
PUBLISHING
INTERNATIONAL

DEDICATION

I dedicate this book to my son, David, my daughter, Grace, my nephew, Elisha and my niece, Esther.

Love

ACKNOWLEDGEMENTS

I would like to thank Bob Proctor who has been my steadfast inspirational light since 2014. His teachings have taught me to live my life by design, and here is his formula in action with my debut book.

Thank you to Peggy McColl, Mick Peterson, Justin Spizman, and my editor, David Ord who have been phenomenal mentors in helping me envision my dream as an author. Thank you for your guidance, patience and friendship.

I would like to thank Judy and her team at Hasmark Publishing International for helping me publish this book.

Thank you Pashmina P. for being my friend and creative connection. Thank you for believing in my story. It is truly remarkable to find another Asian woman writer who sees my vision.

Thank you to my impeccable colleagues, Reverend Dr. Steve Hong, Dr Warren Washington and George Fisher. Thank you for believing in my journey. You make my daily life at "the office" inspiring.

I would especially like to thank Dr. Bruce Victor who diligently gave me immaculate feedback on my writing. I am forever grateful for his patience and especially his knowledge about storytelling. Thank you for listening to me when I needed your guidance, and for reading my entire transcript two or three times. Thank you for your time.

My family, without you I would not be here today. Legacy is so important for sustaining culture and memories. My son and daughter, David and Grace Lee. My brother and sister-in-law, Peter and Marissa and their three children who ignite all of our lives.

And to the Lord or Source above, thank you for all of the opportunities you have presented to me thus far on my path of life. I'm ready for more!

FOREWORD

Written by
Bob Proctor

Many years ago, I had a friend, Clarence Smithison, who had an indefinable spark that made him one of the most remarkable individuals I have ever had the pleasure of knowing. In an attempt to identify this elusive quality, I came to realize that Clarence chose to let his life be guided by faith. He believed that by letting go and letting God, all things become possible.

Guided by her mother's spiritual steadfastness and courage, Christine Lee leads her life by that same guiding principle: she has faith that whatever must happen for her to achieve a goal will indeed occur. As you read Christine's moving tribute to her mother, you will see that it is a beautiful way to live.

Christine came from humble beginnings in Korea. Her mother was sickly; her father was abusive and mostly absent, and she received low grades in school. Nothing about Christine's upbringing signaled that she would become a person to be reckoned with. However, by practicing forgiveness, tuning into the laws of the universe, and "planting good seeds," Christine began to follow her heart and consciously build the life that she loves one choice at a time.

Then, one day, out of the blue, her calling became clear.

While this calling was something Christine had no experience with or had never considered, she knew it was meant for her. And although her mind shifted between excitement and sheer fear, she went for it.

By leaping into a great unknown, Christine currently lives a life that she never imagined was possible for her. And she is happier than she has ever been.

I get really jazzed when I meet people who are living their dream. Having been privileged to work with Christine over the years, I know her to be a person of strong faith and that she has, indeed, received what the masses think is impossible.

If you're tired of letting past or current circumstances dictate your life ... if you're not sure what you really want in life ... or if you have a goal that you're scared to pursue, read *My Hero* from start to finish. As you read, a sense of hope and joy will begin to envelop your heart and soul, and you'll begin to experience perfect harmony, synchronicity, and unlimited creativity.

The universe operates by law. The changes in Christine's life weren't lucky breaks—they were utterly predictable. When you focus on what you want (i.e., live from the inside out) and continually take steps in that direction, you too will realize your dreams, just as Christine has.

I want to leave you with a quote from Clarence Smithison that I refer to often. He said, "Faith is the ability to see the invisible and believe in the incredible, and that is what enables believers to receive what the masses think is impossible."

— **Bob Proctor,**
Bestselling Author of *You Were Born Rich*

CONTENTS

Introduction xiii

1. A Love Letter to My Mother 1
   * A Bridge Between What We Think and What We Do . 3
   * How Our Intuition Speaks to Us 5

2. The Path to the Garden 10
   * Humble Beginnings in a Faraway Land 10
   * My Mother's Early Life 13
   * An Absentee Father 14
   * Childhood Memories 15
   * A Lesson in Tough Love 17
   * A Different Kind of Child 21
   * "You Are Traitors!" 22
   * A Lone Christian Family 25
   * Divided by Religion 27
   * A Fear of Idols 30
   * A Garden of Love 32
   * A Teenage Rebel 35
   * Not a Dunce After All! 38

3. Arriving in the Garden of Hope. 42

- An Immigrant's Story 42
- Forgiving the Unforgivable. 45
- Kicked Out of House and Home. 48
- A Mother's Example Makes All the Difference 50
- A Model of Spiritual Steadfastness 52
- "It's in God's Hands Now". 54
- Getting in Tune with the Laws of the Universe. . . . 57
- Planting Good Seeds. 60

4. Discovering My Calling 63

- A New Purpose Reveals Itself. 63
- A Reason for Being Here. 64
- My Work Was Cut Out for Me 68
- My Mentor Sets Me Straight. 71

To My Mother 76

My Mother's Favorite Scriptures 77

About the Author. .85

INTRODUCTION

Imagine a rocky, winding, pebbled path extending longer than the eye can see. As you take your first step, you feel the small pebbles shift under your feet. They spread to the left and to the right, as if to engulf your shoes. The little rocks steady themselves, and you shift your weight forward, moving your left foot in front of your right. You have arrived at the path to the garden.

A sense of hope envelops your heart and soul. The comfort you feel is overwhelming, as if you have been here before. Although this is your first visit, you are somehow no stranger to the place where you stand. In fact, you have been dreaming about this exact place and time forever.

Time and time again, you find yourself seeing the same image—that of a perfect garden with beautiful flowers of every size and color. Big flowers, little flowers, all resting close to one another as if they were created to coexist.

This perfectly balanced and wonderfully assorted garden is the place of your dreams—and here you are, about to enter it. There is no place you'd rather be. It offers perfect harmony, synchronicity, and unlimited creativity.

While you are just a visitor, one of many, you feel as if you are home. As you swiftly place one foot in front of the other stepping closer to the garden, you close your eyes and imagine what awaits you at the end of this path. You can visualize it before you even arrive. This is *your* garden, and you are humbly progressing along the path to arrive there.

For much of my life, this garden seemed very far away. But even at a young age, I knew I would eventually find the place that I could only ever see in my dreams. This beautiful garden was a responsibility that was all my own.

While it was awaiting me at the end of the rocky road, it was a garden I had been to time and time again. It was me who picked and pruned and cared for each flower in this garden. It was my garden of life, carefully curated by each decision, thought, action, and seedling of love I could offer.

The journey to creating this garden began late in 1961, in a far-away place.

1

A LOVE LETTER TO
MY MOTHER

Famed physicist, thinker and all-around game changer Albert Einstein said it best: "The only real valuable thing is intuition."

As you journey through life, have there been moments where you knew something was true, or you knew that you should take a particular action, even though you had no evidence that your conclusion was accurate? It didn't matter what you were told, how you viewed things, or what others might say. Your heart and soul understood the truth as clear as day. This immediate and overwhelming feeling is what I call *intuition*. It's a deep-seated *knowing*—a strong sensation that acts as a keen insight. I have come to understand that we often ignore intuition at our own peril.

A classic dictionary definition of *intuition* is the ability to acquire knowledge without proof, evidence, or conscious reasoning. Just think of the power of that!

It's as if you can take a short cut in life, coming to conclusions without putting in the legwork. You need no tangible proof, because something in you already knows the truth.

"I define intuition as the subtle knowing without ever having any idea why you know it," says Sophy Burnham, bestselling author of *The Art of Intuition*. "It's different from thinking, it's different from logic or analysis. It's a knowing without knowing."

We are at a time in history when many are learning to allow their intuition to guide their lives, and that's a good thing. Until recently, only a minority of people were guided by their intuition. Across the ages, most people didn't even recognize their intuition when it was speaking to them. If you cannot trust your own version of the truth, then what or who can you trust?

I was fortunate to have a one-in-a-million mother. Through thick and thin, no matter how defiant or rebellious I was in my earlier years, she stuck with me. Her exemplary life, unmatched love, adoration of Jesus Christ, and great wisdom taught me what it means to live a purposeful life. I learned the difference between just floating through life under the influence of others, and allowing my intuition to become my North Star.

Throughout my own life, many of the successful decisions I made were the direct result of my intuition. Having a mother tutor me like mine did, I now know to not ignore an insight when it comes to me. On the contrary, I embrace it. I listen to it and allow it to act as my guiding light.

There was a time when I didn't always follow my intuition, and I'll expand on that in later chapters. But I discovered that it was always a mistake to ignore what my inner being was saying to me. Even though all the signs were clearly in front of me, I turned the other way and relied on far weaker signals. As you can imagine, when I did this, things didn't always work out so well.

As reliable as our intuition is, thinking we are in touch with it can like be like a double-edged sword. If we mistake our ego for our intuition, which I'll explain as we proceed, we can go in the wrong direction altogether—sometimes disastrously so. In such situations, we make decisions based on a faulty compass. However, if our intuition is *truly* our own intuition and we trust it fully, the sky is the limit.

When we come to a fork in the road, it's especially important to tune into this deeper part of ourselves. As HuffPost's founder Arianna Huffington tells us in her book *Thrive,* "Even when we're not at a fork in the road, wondering what to do and trying to hear that inner voice, our intuition is always there, always reading the situation, always trying to steer us the right way."

A Bridge Between What We Think and What We Do

God has given each of us an internal compass. As we focus on this intuitive aspect of ourselves, we sharpen our minds and create a bridge of trust between what we think and what we do. This bridge is our intuition, which should be sturdy and reliable.

A great article in the Huffington Post outlines what people who are in touch with their intuition do differently from others:

- They listen to their inner voices.
- They take time for solitude.
- They create.
- They practice mindfulness.
- They observe everything around them.
- They listen to their bodies.

- They connect deeply with others.
- They pay attention to their dreams.
- They enjoy plenty of down time.
- They consciously let go of negative emotions.

Do you practice these important skills? If so, you are clearly in touch with your intuition, and this connection likely plays an important role in your success. People who make sound decisions waste little time belaboring choices and generally move in the direction of their life goals.

If for whatever reason you find that you aren't checking all the above boxes, then you likely aren't maximizing your ability to utilize your intuition. Intuition is a powerful expression of direction that is available to us at no cost. We are all born with some level of intuition, though what we decide to do with it is a choice that's all our own.

As my story unfolds over the course of this book, you will see how my intuition was continuously developed, largely due to my mother's devotion to my wellbeing. Little by little, she taught me to rely on my inner being. When I screwed up, she allowed me to learn lessons the hard way. Thankfully I got the point, and I came to rely on my intuition to the point that small miracles began to appear in the most ordinary aspects of daily life. I'll tell you more about that as we proceed.

This book was originally conceived as a love letter to my mother. It has been twenty years since she departed this life, but over the years the lessons she taught me have increasingly come to fruition. As I began to write that love letter, I realized there were many insights that I wanted to make available to others. Eventually, the love letter turned into this book. Much of what I share comes from my mother, who was a prayer warrior like none I have ever known. In every aspect of her life, she lived her faith to the maximum, requiring courage and a boldness in situations that at times threatened her wellbeing and that of her family.

From the time that she was a young child, my mother was afflicted with a health issue that stayed with her until she transitioned to the heavenly plane at the age of sixty-five. But unlike so many, she didn't see life as a trial that we simply have to survive; she believed in the goodness of God and embraced the words of Jesus, "I have come that they may have life, and that they may have it more abundantly."

God doesn't change our essential makeup or the environment into which we are born, but as you will see from my story, he gives us the grace to live an abundant life. Through Jesus, my mother's spirit triumphed spectacularly. She was not guided by her ego, but by her essential being, which she realized bore the image and likeness of the divine. My life has increasingly become empowered by the same intuition that guided my mother throughout her entire life.

How Our Intuition Speaks to Us

I find that people want to know how to identify their intuition, given how easy it is for our ego to fool us.

The issue of how our intuition communicates with us is a bit of a trick question in some regards. This is because our intuition isn't separate from us. As I have already indicated, it's an aspect of our deepest self. Since we are each a unique expression of the Source of all wisdom, insight doesn't come to us—it arises *within* us as a kind of "inner knowing." This is what it means to be guided by the Holy Spirit, which Jesus referred to as our ever-present counselor.

Our intuition speaks to us in "a still small voice." We have likely all heard this expression, but what does it mean?

We are urged to listen for and listen to this voice. However, this can be somewhat misleading. It isn't a voice that we are listening for in the way we listen for another person to speak to us. It's not an audible voice that we seek to hear.

The expression "a still small voice" comes from the life of a Hebrew prophet. If there's one thing I learned from my mother, it's how important some of the biblical insights are for our daily lives. At the end of this book, I'll share some of her favorite scriptures.

The prophet Elijah was going through a tough time in his life and longed for God to appear to him. In the end, his dream came true—but not in the way he was expecting.

Humans have long tended to associate the divine with dramatic events in nature. The story of Elijah offers us a different insight into how God is revealed to us. Discouraged, Elijah wanted God to appear and reassure him that he was on the right track. He's told to stand on the mountain to which he has journeyed. Then the drama begins.

First there is a wind—perhaps a tornado or hurricane—so powerful that it sends rocks crashing down. Following the windstorm, there is an earthquake. You might think of it as a symbol of those times when our lives feel totally shaken up. After the earthquake comes a firestorm, like a huge fireworks display of lightning. In none of these does God appear to Elijah.

Only when the drama is over does Elijah perceive the divine presence, which comes in the form of what the traditional translation describes as "a still small voice." I like the way the New Revised Standard Version of the Bible expresses this idea, because I think it gives the sense more accurately. There came "a sound of sheer silence."

The expression "a sound of sheer silence" points to the absolute stillness in which the infinite mystery we call God abides. It equates to what a later writer in the Christian tradition speaks of as "the peace of God, which surpasses all understanding."

The "sound of sheer silence" refers to the essence of our being, where there is a silence that is filled with divine consciousness. This is the source of our intuition—our inner *knowing*.

The insight we experience when our intuition is guiding us comes as a felt knowing that can't necessarily be explained because it's a part of us. It's similar to how we can't find our "self" by seeking to identify an objective reality inside ourselves. Think of how the eye can't see itself unless it looks in a mirror.

In our still center, we are beyond form. We are part of the formless infinite out of which everything arises. From this formless state, all forms come into existence, together with all the experiences that form is capable of having.

To access our intuition, all we are required to do is become still. We don't even have to chase our myriad thoughts out of our head; we simply observe our monkey mind as it dishes them up. There's a fundamental difference between forcing the mind to be quiet and relaxing into the stillness, the emptiness, the formlessness of divine consciousness.

If you try to still your mind, you'll likely find it a futile mission. This is because the practice is likely to be an effort of the ego. Our ego loves the hard way, the painful way, the heavy burden. Accustomed to suffering as most of us are, all of this effort keeps the ego from having to dissolve into the stillness of simply *being*.

If we relax into the stillness within, we find that our mind becomes not just peaceful, but profoundly alert. We are simultaneously at peace with ourselves and deeply aware. Even the briefest experience of stillness is like a taste of honey, and we want to experience more of it. We want the frequency and length of our times of stillness to increase until inner stillness becomes our abiding state even when we are extremely active.

American Alpine ski racer Diane Roffe-Steinrotter captured a second gold medal in the 1994 Winter Olympics. Asked about her experience, she remarked that she remembered nothing about the race other than—you'll hardly believe the expression she used— other than "being immersed in *relaxation*."

This is the state Jesus pointed to when he said, "Out of your innermost being will *flow rivers of living water*." Do you know how Diane Roffe-Steinrotter described the state she was in as she raced for her second gold? She recalls, "I felt like a *waterfall*."

Post-impressionist painter Paul Cezanne described this same feeling as an artist: "Right now a moment of time is fleeting by! Capture its reality in paint! To do that we must put all else out of our

minds. We must become that moment, make ourselves a sensitive recording plate."

On the eightieth birthday of acclaimed Italian conductor Arturo Toscanini, someone asked his son Walter what his father ranked as his most important achievement. The son replied, "For him there can be no such thing. Whatever he happens to be doing at the moment is the biggest thing in his life—whether it is conducting a symphony, or simply peeling an orange." This is what it's like to live in the state of flow Jesus spoke of.

These introductory thoughts are ones that help me focus on my present level of intuition. You might also wish to take a moment and connect with your inner being, allowing your intuition to speak to you. Focus your thoughts on building the bridge of trust between what you think and what you do. Once you build it, try to cross it often, as it will most certainly help you travel in the direction of your ultimate goal.

This is what my mother did, and in so many ways it changed the course of her life (and ultimately my own) to one of abundance despite her ill health.

2

THE PATH TO THE GARDEN

Humble Beginnings in a Faraway Land

Situations that plunge us into emotional turmoil have the potential to awaken us to an aspect of ourselves of which we are unaware. They alert us to where our inner being is seeking to blossom in a particular dimension of our lives.

Early in my life, I began to encounter a daring courage within myself that mirrored that of my mother's. In due time, this courage would become a key element of my life's purpose. Even at a young age, I was a girl with a sense of bravery and strength that didn't match my petite stature. Small as I was, very little frightened me. In time, this would become a key aspect of how I dealt with the world around me.

I began to discover this aspect of myself after an incident involving our village drunk. He seemed to be inebriated pretty much all the time, and he took pleasure in abusing his poor wife on the street in front of the entire village. It had become his regular daily practice.

When I was five years old, I happened to be passing by and observed the terror on the woman's face. The villagers stood around watching. When no one intervened to stop the assault, I became furious. The violence went on and on, so I decided to stand up for this poor woman.

Finding a stick that was taller than myself, I raised it in the air and prepared to swing it at the drunk.

Striding bravely toward him, I yelled, "Stop this right now! If you don't, I'll hit you with this stick and hurt you badly. What has your wife done that gives you the right to beat her like this? If I see you drunk and laying a finger on her again, you're going to be really sorry!"

I could hardly believe my own actions. I don't know where the courage came from to challenge this man. The crowd could hardly believe what they were witnessing: a tiny five-year-old girl with a four-foot stick ready to beat the drunk man senseless.

The man stopped striking his wife. The villagers were amazed, and everyone dispersed to their homes. After that encounter, I never once saw the man harm his wife again.

I had inherited my mother's courage. My mother had married my father after meeting him at Dongdochun in South Korea, where she worked as a tailor. Following my father's middle school years, he worked for the American army as a translator. My mother's education hadn't gone beyond K1. She was twenty-three years old when they met. My father found her to be a sweet and respectful young woman. He was especially attracted by her innocence and sincerity.

My father turned out to be a workaholic, and was absent a lot. He had little regard for his wife or his children. As time went on, I had to take his place in the family, giving due diligence to my mother, my brothers, and my sister.

I was born December 23, 1961, in the midst of a harsh South Korean winter. As the snow pounded the small city of Chungchungnamdo, my sickly mother brought me into the world. I was her fourth child, and the third daughter in the family.

My mother's sickly state also affected me during my early years. I was a weak and feeble child who weighed a mere five pounds at birth.

My entry into the world evoked little excitement in my immediate family. Nothing about my birth gave a hint that I would soon become someone to be reckoned with.

Shortly after my birth, my mother returned to work on the family farm. To ensure that we had food on the table, much of the time it seemed she was working at the farm day and night. Her dogged determination kept our family afloat at a particularly difficult time in South Korea. It was from my mother's bravery in the face of adversity that I learned to be courageous. No child could have a more perfect model of what dedication involves than the example my mother set for her children.

Because I was chubby and my eyes were a deep brown color, in elementary school I quickly earned the nickname "night owl." But an owl notices every movement, and my mother had engendered in me a sense that there was a purpose for my life. Instead of accepting the station in life that society wished to assign me, she also taught me to find my own place in the world. This is why I challenged the village drunk in the way I did.

My Mother's Early Life

It will help if I share with you how difficult life was for my mother when she was young, since I believe this formed the basis of her courage. For thirty-six years, Korea was colonized by Japan. Any authentic Korean customs or traditions had to take place strictly behind closed doors. This was an extremely dark time for my homeland—and for my mother especially, since it largely fell on her to provide for and protect us.

When my mother turned twelve, Japanese soldiers came to the village searching for every ounce of gold they could find, and collecting other minerals as well. They even stole the villagers' rice. They searched each house, and if they found any sort of arms, they burned the dwelling and killed its occupants.

My mother was beautiful when she was young. Since her father was gone much of the time, it fell to my uncle to hide her as long as he could, or she would have been raped by Japanese soldiers. As she continued to grow into a teen, he realized he needed to resort to drastic measures to protect her. He chose a Korean mill cutter (a long knife) and handicapped my mother's ankles. Badly bloodied, for a while my mother couldn't walk. Since soldiers weren't interested in anyone who was handicapped, my uncle's actions ensured she wasn't taken by soldiers and used as a "comfort woman." Her wounded ankles and legs handicapped her for the rest of her life.

The Japanese had a huge impact on Korea, and many Koreans changed their names to Japanese names. Teaching of the Korean language was forbidden, resulting in much Korean culture being lost. It wasn't until the bombing of Hiroshima and Nagasaki, which forced Japan's emperor to surrender, that Korea again became a free country.

During the Second World War, most Koreans were unable to reach out to a doctor, a pharmacist, or a clinic. My mother was in her thirties at the time. The lack of skilled medical attention affected her health. Already suffering from illness, it was during this period that her severe shortness of breath began, taking a toll on her that would be with her for the rest of her life. Breathing became difficult not only during the day, but especially at night. At times, she coughed endlessly throughout the night. My father was gone much of the time, so she had no support. I often cried for my mother as I witnessed the difficult times that she was going through.

An Absentee Father

My mother wasn't a person who normally shed tears. But one day when I was three or four years old, she received a telegram that caused her to weep. She learned that her mother, my grandmother, had suddenly passed away. My mother had counted on being able to see her before she died. Determined to travel to Yesan for the funeral, my mother desperately needed a babysitter. Thankfully, a member of the church we attended offered to take care of us.

This was a tough time for all of us. I think of my grandmother today and miss her. In the end, through many tears, my mother accepted the loss, filling the gap in her life by stepping up her service to God.

Even though my father was absent much of the time and abused my mother when he was home, she never sought out a different husband to replace him. She had committed to be with him for life. Instead, early each morning she rose to pray from three to four o'clock. She found comfort in her spirituality. I am forever grateful that she is the one who brought me into the world, as well as for all that she taught me about what dedication to God truly means.

While I missed my father, I eventually became grateful that he was gone. One evening while he was home, I overheard sounds of violence from the other room. I was asleep at the time, and first thought I must be dreaming.

Opening my eyes, I got out of bed and entered my parents' room. I couldn't believe what I encountered: my father was beating my mother, punching her on all sides.

When I realized my father wasn't going to stop his assault, out of shock I shouted at him, "Stop! Stop! You bastard. Do not hurt my mom ever again!" As with the village drunk, I was only five years old at the time, but seeing my father beat my mother made me as mad as hell. I warned him, "How can you even be my dad? If I see you hit my mom again, I will beat the crap out of you."

Childhood Memories

Our village was called Bamgul, which means "snake village." Its name came from the fact that the village people worshiped snakes as gods. The snake acted like a spiritual security guard and was said to protect families from bad luck.

I once stayed overnight at my uncle's house. In the morning, I saw a huge snake descending from the roof. I was terrified. My uncle and his wife advised, "Don't worry about the snake. Don't even chase it away. Its dragon-like character protects our home and family." I watched this reptile move freely among the *jangdokdae*, which are types of Korean food jars. Suddenly it disappeared. My uncle believed the snake was sent by God. Based on shamanism, such was the nonsense that my uncle and his wife subscribed to.

The incident caused me to appreciate the fact that my mother was a devoted Christian. She used to keep our family safe by chasing snakes away, or if necessary, by killing them. I think back to times when snakes appeared as she cooked in the kitchen or worked at the farm. She was never afraid of them, instead putting her trust in God.

I appreciated my mother's faith because, as Christians, death was an event we talked openly about. At times, I used to play with a friend named Mi Kyung. We also went to church together, although her mother wasn't a Christian. Her mother was a little person, and very pretty.

When I was six or seven years old, Mi Kyung's mother suddenly passed away.

Since no one told Mi that her mother had died, in the days following her mother's death, Mi searched for her. When the *sangru*, a vehicle that transported coffins, pulled up at the house, it was decorated with many flowers so Mi tried to ride it. She had no idea that it was there to take her mother to her funeral. Since there were no doctors in the area, no one really knew why she passed away. I thought to myself. "How lucky I am to have my mother, with her devotion to God."

While I was a pupil at Chungso elementary school, we walked four hours to Dimimong, a famous shoreline village along the western shore. Here, we would enjoy a treasure hunt. There was also a large playground for picnicking, and we all looked forward to bathing in the sea. We especially enjoyed the way the waves rolled in so strongly, then at times receded to the point we could see the sea bottom. People were keen to jump into the sea so they could fish for crabs and perhaps find pearls.

At times, we stayed in the park for up to four hours. I remember some villagers combing the seabed until the last minute gathering as much fish as they could. The waves would then come roaring in. At times, some found themselves cut off by the sudden return of the tide. A few even died because their way of escape was blocked.

On our trips to Dimimong, I used to arise early to be at the school around six in the morning. On such occasions, one hour of the day was set aside for eating lunch. I didn't bring any lunch with me because I didn't want my mother to go to such trouble when her health was so bad. Instead, I went to the picnic on an empty stomach, and I was happy to do so because I loved my mother dearly. I tried not to be a burden, not even as a young child. We would return to school, another four-hour walk, making sure we arrived before the sun was down.

On Sunday mornings, even if it had been a stormy night with gale-force winds or heavy rain, my mother was up at three o'clock in the morning. She lit the oil lamp and carried me on her back as we walked to church in the dark. I was very attached to her. She was my reason for taking my next breath. Sometimes the moon was out, guiding our footsteps. She was a truly dedicated, disciplined, and beautiful human being.

A Lesson in Tough Love

My mother also understood the importance of tough love. One of the worst choices I made as a young girl occurred much earlier in my life. I was probably six years old and in first grade.

There used to be a shop called Chungso by the entrance to my elementary school. They sold notebooks, pens, pencils, and candy. One day they had yellow duck dolls, along with other dolls. I wanted a yellow duck doll so badly that I couldn't sleep. I was afraid that the last doll would disappear if I didn't purchase one soon. I didn't have the courage to tell my mother how much I wanted the doll, since I was afraid that she would say we couldn't afford it. This was when I decided to ignore my intuition and do something really stupid.

While my mother was asleep, I stole twenty-five won, the equivalent of five cents. I had always been afraid to put my hands in her *sokchima*, which was the kind of dress Korean women wore inside the house in the 1960s. It was incredibly exciting to finally have the money to purchase the yellow duck doll. I bought it and stuffed it into my backpack.

On the way home, I became afraid that my mother would discover that I had stolen her money. I decided to run away to a classmate's house, even though they lived far away in the mountains. It took me almost a half day to walk there. I had heard that tigers and lions at times loitered on the track, so I hoped I wouldn't meet any of them and end up being eaten! I decided to run. When I reached my friend's house, I was so exhausted that all I could do was sleep. After returning to school the next day, my cousin's sibling informed me that my mom was so worried and had gone out looking for me. I knew I was in big trouble. Scared to death, I didn't know what to do. In the end, I decided to go back home and confess.

When I arrived home, my mom had six or seven mulberry tree sticks and made me pull my pants down. The stick was incredibly painful and left marks on both my legs. Six of the eight sticks were broken as she punished me. I begged my mother to forgive me, crying so hard and swearing that I would never steal again. I couldn't walk for two or three days. I was locked in a room by myself in order to contemplate how much danger I had put myself in.

My mother explained that God hands out tough lessons until we get the point. If we refuse to learn, the lessons get tougher. After this, I never thought of taking another person's property again.

The beating my mother gave me for stealing her money wasn't the only severe beating I received. When I entered middle school, I think I must have inherited some of my mother's traits, since school life didn't interest me. I remember being the dumbest student in the class. I could never get beyond a D grade in any subject. In my seventh and eighth grades, out of fifty-five classmates, I was an F student. I had little understanding of what was being taught, and I wasn't the least bit interested.

A friend and I were always competing with one another. The two of us were at the bottom of the class. Her name was Park Sang Poong, and she always sat next to me. We were assigned to clean the floors after class and organize the classroom. It was our job to clean the windows, pick up the trash in the playground, and run any errands requested by the teachers.

When I was in K3 through K9, I used to hide my grades or lie about them. The letters D or F were always on my report card (which also said I couldn't read, needed to catch up, was too slow, had a learning disability, was a rebel, and didn't do my homework). I either hid the report card or, before I gave it to my parents, changed the F grades to a C or B+.

One day, I arrived home and knew something was wrong. My brother and sister looked at me as if to say, "poor you." I didn't know that the school counselor had been in contact with my parents. My father was home at the time and waiting for me with a thick stick. My mother told me to tell my father, "I confess I have done wrong by hiding or changing my report card." My father locked the door to his room and started to ask me questions about school. I didn't know what to say.

On this occasion, unlike with the duck doll earlier in life, there was a reason for my irrational behavior. My father had been gone so much, he felt like a stranger. At that time, he was working, though he only supported the family to a degree that our finances were always tight. My mother's health also continued to deteriorate. Her asthma prevented her from working at the sewing factory downtown, since her affliction worsened as a result of the dusty factory environment. Also, she already had a hard enough life without taking the bus to and from work each day. We had visited the emergency department where the doctor confirmed that she shouldn't be working at the clothing factory.

It was a real pity that my mother couldn't work in the clothing industry. Ever since she was young, she had shown promise as a tailor. In our village, everyone wore her hats, which were fashioned in the style of traditional Korean clothing. From a young age, she used her talent to support the family. The entire village loved her handmade clothes because they were measured particularly for each person. There was no electricity in Korea during the 1950s and 1960s, so there were no sewing machines. While my mother was sewing, she used an oil lamp to work deep into the night. Although her tailoring was exemplary, she was entirely self-taught.

Not enjoying school at all, I decided I would rather work to support my mother. Consequently, I ditched school and began working for a dry cleaner to boost our family's income. When I tried to explain this to my father, he wasn't interested in my excuses. He hit me with the stick until it finally broke. My legs were bleeding so badly that, as had happened when I was young, again I couldn't walk for the next several days. I had only wanted to do something to assist my family, especially my mother.

Because my mother wasn't supported by her husband most of the time, her days were far from easy. Not only did she lose three of her own children, but her health was now growing visibly worse.

A Different Kind of Child

Remembering back to when I was younger, my mother was worried that I was different from my siblings, so she made me sleep by her side. One day when I was in K2, a classmate teased me in front of everyone: "I hear you still sleep with your mom and pee on the blanket! You're still a baby! You should grow up if you intend to come to school."

I was so embarrassed that I threw a rock at him. "It's not true," I said as tears welled up in my eyes. One of my classmates was called Dosan. He was the doctor's son. The doctor manned the clinic, which offered the immunizations required for elementary school.

My mother used to take me to Dosan's father. I used to hate shots. The idea of a shot scared me so much that I ran to a nearby village. Finally, my mother, the doctor, and the nurse grabbed me and administered the shot, my tears notwithstanding. I have to admit that I liked the fact I was given a candy afterwards, since it was one of my favorites—a big red ball-shaped candy.

When I received the shot, I realized that my classmate Dosan was watching from behind the curtain. He was a quiet boy. I discovered that his mother and father were divorced because his father was having an affair with his nurse. Oh, how lucky I was to have a mother such as mine!

My mother was tough and told me, "You have to be tough to serve God. We are the army of God, and our primary task it to serve him and protect his kingdom."

"You Are Traitors!"

The translated name of our village was "Rocky Snake village." One of my scariest moments from childhood was when the people of our village came to our home intent on firebombing it. It's one of my earliest memories from before I started elementary school. We were terrified that this would be our family's last day on earth. This was back in the 1960s, and we were the only Christian family in the village.

Only later did I find out that this incident occurred because someone said that a North Korean spy was living in our house. Rumor spread that our family was the enemy of South Korea.

The rumor began during one of the times when my father was away overseas and there wasn't a man in our house to protect us. The villagers were determined that we should be removed from the village. If we didn't go voluntarily, they would make us go by burning our house.

Later, we found out that two sons of my uncle had been backstabbing my father, calling him a spy for North Korea. They were jealous that my father was so successful as a leader of *Saemaeul Undong*, a South Korean revolution headed up by President Patk Jung Hee.

Holding her children close, my mother was brave as she began to pray. "God, you are almighty. I am in danger at this moment. Give me strength and wisdom. Let them turn away from the evil that they intend. I bless them for the ignorance of not recognizing that you alone are God."

Just like that, the crowds dispersed as if nothing had happened. Later the neighbors apologized for the misunderstanding. My mother was so sincere that several people became her friends; some began to attend Sunday worship with us.

When I was about six years old and living in Sadong with my mother, brother, and sister, my father came from Vietnam to visit us for a couple of months before going back again to work with the U.S. Army. The year was 1967. While he was at home, my uncle's two sons came back to our home, kidnapped my father, and took him to the mountain behind our village. Jealous of his success, their intention was to kill him. Feeling powerless, my mother was shocked. She started praying, asking God to intervene. Thankfully, my father survived and was released without harm. My mother's faith in God prevailed yet again.

This wasn't the only time we faced danger. Once we traveled to my mother's younger brother's house at Norabgjin, a journey that took six hours by train. As soon as we arrived and got off the train, three men surrounded us. We were trapped, but my mother told them bravely, "You guys can't take me or my kids. My brother works for the police station that guards this platform and is looking for me right now!" She pointed at the police station, then grabbed the hands of my brother Ian and myself, holding us tight to her chest. The intruders suddenly ran. I later found out that they were engaged in human trafficking. If it weren't for my mother's bravery, we would have been taken and sold as sex slaves.

My uncle was the younger brother of my mother and happened to be working at the train station that day. Tragically, he died at a young age as the result of an accident at the station. I recall how my mother went through some truly sad moments after his death.

Not only was my mother's bravery inspiring, but her generosity was well known. This was the period after the Korean war, a time when our country struggled because it was now divided between North and South. A lot of families were separated, which spurred a great deal of personal and economic unrest. Many tears were shed during this time, and no one knew what tomorrow would bring.

During this period, I encountered people who were rendered homeless by the war, especially in small villages such as the one we lived in. We were middle-class, and my family's inheritance included a farm. We were not rich, but we had what we needed. My mother greeted anyone who was destitute with full bowls of rice and several side dishes. She wanted no one to go hungry.

When someone left our home, my mother loaded them up with a bag of rice, either to use themselves or to share with others. It was extremely important for her to ensure their immediate needs were met.

During my entire life, I never once saw my mother turn down a person in need. She was one of the most welcoming and loving people I have ever encountered.

Our house was always filled with people from the church, as well as members of the pastor's family. They came to our home to sing and enjoy Bible studies.

At this time, we lived with another of my uncles who was handicapped. Despite his handicap, he helped my mother with her farming as much as he possibly could. When her days ran late, he babysat us and performed various chores around the house. My mother was infinitely patient with him, always willing to offer a gentle and caring hand as he struggled with his disability.

A Lone Christian Family

My mother's courage showed up in many ways, one of which was the fact that we were the only Christian family in our village. My mother had converted to Christianity while married to my father, since her grandmother on my father's side had become a Christian in the 1950s. One day my grandmother decided to become Buddhist. This brought her Christian years to an end, which precipitated a major problem for my mother.

Today, I understand the family's attraction to Buddhism. When I was twelve years old, I was fascinated by Buddhism and had a hankering to become a monk. I felt a calling deep within me that seemed to emerge from my very soul.

There was a Buddhist temple in the mountains, not far from my middle school. To me, the temple was so attractive. It appealed to a side of myself that I didn't understand at the time. Given that my family was Christian and my mother was a powerful prayer warrior, I couldn't easily take the step of changing my religious allegiance.

I wanted to tell my mother of my leanings, but this was impossible. She would have died had she known that I wanted to become a monk! I loved her so deeply that I didn't wish to disturb her sense of wellbeing. Eventually, I settled on being a monk "in my heart." Only years later did I come to see that, given the chaotic nature of my life, it was the peacefulness of monks that I sought, not their sparse lifestyle. When we lived in the small South Korean village of Chungcundo, our house was a small shanty filled to the brim with people and animals. We had two cows, four pigs, fifteen chickens, and two dogs. It was not a peaceful atmosphere for a child like me. I only found the peacefulness I sought by developing a personal relationship with Jesus Christ.

When the rest of the family turned to Buddhism, my mother was appalled at the idea of worshiping idols. She simply couldn't agree with this. Because her Christian faith was so deeply rooted, nothing the family did could get her to renegotiate her beliefs. She had four siblings—three brothers and one stepsister. Until now, she had enjoyed a good relationship with the wider family. They had always been respectful of us, welcoming us into their homes. However, the change from Christianity to Buddhism had a severe impact on our family's unity.

I recall the day one of my uncles called on us. His visit led to my mother being treated in an abusive manner. The Korean people celebrate *Jaesae* twice each year, once at *chusuk* (Korean Thanksgiving) and the other occasion being *Saehae* (Korean calendar new year). The festival has been a part of Korean culture for over two-thousand years. This is a time when families come together to enjoy the best food, as well as to play games such as *Yuknore*.

Throughout the festival, Koreans wear beautiful traditional clothing known as *Hanbok*. The celebration lasts from three to five days.

This should have been an occasion when my mother's family rallied around her, since it always reminded her of a painful time in her life. Before I was born, my mother lost two young children as a result of these festivities. During Jaesae, people are prone to drinking alcohol. My two sisters somehow got into a bottle of an alcoholic beverage known as *Soju*. When it was discovered, they were already severely ill. It was too late to rush them to a doctor since there were no doctors, or even a clinic, in our village in the 1950s. Both girls became poisoned from the alcohol.

The New Year, known as *Saehae*, is a time when the males of the family are accustomed to bowing three times to each of the family members who have passed, such as our grandmother and grandfather. Even though it was only men who took part in the ceremony, it irked the family that my mother didn't agree with their customary bowing. As a result, my mother wasn't permitted to attend the New Year celebrations and was banished to the kitchen for several days to prepare the repast for everyone else. As a result of her continued adherence to her Christian faith, she was treated as if she was a slave.

Divided by Religion

The abuse of my mother eventually erupted in a showdown, the result of which was that she was kicked out of my grandmother's house several times. She was only allowed to enter the house again because she was pregnant. The family had it in mind to take charge of her forthcoming addition to the family.

The uncle, who was the younger brother of the family, was the worst. He spread lies about my mother, always backstabbing her. They mocked my mother's service to the church. While my father was away in Vietnam, my uncle claimed that my mother stole from the family and gave the money to the church, enriching the pastor's family while neglecting her own children. This wasn't at all true, but it served to cement the split between my mother and father.

This uncle even suggested in a letter to my father that he should send money to his own bank account, not that of his wife. The reality was that my uncle was stealing my family's money. I found out later that his lies about my mother in letters to my father were the cause of our family's problems. His stealing is why he was able to stay home all the time instead of working. He spent much of his time around our home begging for help.

Some in our family used to come and give my mother a hard time, cursing her, and even physically harming her. One day my father's sister swore that my mother was romantically involved with the church pastor! When my father returned home from working for an American company in Vietnam, I thought he was going to kill my mother. I watched him carefully, and eventually ordered him, "Get out! Don't ever touch my mother again."

One day, my aunt complained that her husband wasn't working and didn't have any desire to get a job. "He isn't responsible," she said. "Please help, sister." My mother asked her to go with her to the church and tried to get her to accept Jesus. "God will provide abundantly for your family," she promised. Then she gave them a bag of rice and some money.

The reality was that this uncle was lazy, demanding, bullying, and two-faced. Despite this, I never saw my mother blame him. She always greeted him with a sincere smile, saying, "How may I help you?"

Then she would suggest, "Let's go to church this Wednesday for Bible study."

My uncle and his wife always replied, "We will go next week because we are busy this Wednesday." Then they wouldn't show up again until they needed more help.

Some thirty years later, I overheard a conversation between my father and my uncle that confirmed what really happened. It turned out that it was indeed my uncle who stole from the family's account.

Generosity and compassion are good. My mother believed in giving, but she gave only from her own money. She always had new, clean money in her Bible, from which she paid her tithes. I never saw her miss paying a tithe once in her entire life. She was a generous donor to the church, and she always helped the homeless to any extent that our supplies would allow.

How privileged I was to be brought up by one of the most generous people I have ever encountered. She was a living angel, always about God's work. This was her way of showing God how grateful she was. She was never arrogant or complaining. She was in many ways both a pastor and a missionary in her own right. Her character came from a higher dimension.

Today, living in America, I am glad to say that this is a country where I am proud to proclaim to the world, "I am a Christian who also loves devotees of Islam, Buddhists, Hindus, Sikhs, and members of other faiths." The division that occurred in our family was quite unnecessary. Each should be allowed to follow the path their hearts lead them on, as we are free to do in the United States.

How my mother responded to others as the only Christian in her family, and in fact in our entire village, was inspiring. Even though everyone turned against her and treated her in abusive ways, she never retaliated. When people refused to treat her with civility, she continued to be kind to them regardless. I consider myself fortunate to have a mother who was so loyal to the way Jesus lived.

My mother became devoted to God when she was just twenty-three years old, and she never looked back from this decision. In those days, most Koreans hadn't awakened to the truth of Christianity.

The idea of entering a different paradigm was unimaginable to most. Even though no one supported my mother, and many threw rocks at her, she never wavered in her love for Jesus.

My mother was a visionary in terms of her children's path, but it wasn't an easy path she mapped out for us. She advocated the "no pain, no gain" philosophy of life.

A Fear of Idols

In Korea in the 1960s, there were many idols. It was popular to change your religion in those days, and people adopted different gods with frequency. My mother never had anything to do with idols, choosing to worship only Jesus Christ.

Some of these idols frightened me. One time when we visited my uncle's house, I remember being scared by *Modang*. After this incident, my mother forbode her children from visiting her brother's house. It didn't go down well, and my uncle and my mother basically stopped seeing each other.

Modang has a long history in Korean shamanism, dating back a thousand years. The ceremony features a woman dressed in a colorful Korean dress; the sort of outfit worn by Korean solders a hundred years before. She wears a hat and carries a long knife in one hand, while in the other hand she holds a *Buchae* fan. She then dances on knives made of wood and sharp steel. People flock to hear the messages she delivers from various idols. These messages are known as *Shinrungmin*.

The ceremony takes place in front of the family dwelling. The entire family gathers to pray to Modang, offering prayers of *binaeda*, a word meaning "please." Everyone continues to say "binaeda, binaeda" while seated in a bowed position. The family pleads with the idol to bestow wealth, good luck, and a cure for any sickness in the family.

While two or three individuals play drums and lead the cheering and singing, Modang dances and swings her knife swings all over the place as if she might attack you. She constantly asks for money. Each time you pay, you make a wish. For instance, she might say that your father will be free from disease if you pay her 50,000 won. Modang continues to sing and dance on the sharp knives for two or three hours, as long as the participants continue to pay.

Koreans believe that if they don't listen to Modang, idols will curse the family with bad luck. Modang could be likened to the western idea of witches. This is the sort of nonsense that shamanism and its idols hold over many present-day Koreans.

I look back and think how smart my mother was to embrace Christianity, which has been such a powerful influence in my own life. If it weren't for my mother and her faith, I wouldn't be the person I am today. I don't even give a thought to all the idols people worship back in Korea, for all their worldly glamor. My mother had such a profound effect on my self-image, for which I am so deeply grateful. To show me that I am a child of God was the best gift anyone could ever give me.

A Garden of Love

Even though times were difficult, especially given the rupture in the wider family over religion, my mother nevertheless instilled a sense of love in our home. I still remember the small and beautiful garden she planted in the front of the house; it was a symbol of how much she cared. In the spring, she planted new flowers. I remember coming home each spring day and seeing my mother kneeling down as she worked the soil. She filled the garden with roses, tulips, and *bongsongha* (a beautiful Korean flower).

My mother remains my hero, because in so many ways she was an excellent example of a life grounded in Jesus. She helped me build my own relationship with God. The courage to stand up to the village drunk, and to my father, I learned from my mother's own courageousness. She showed me how important it is to stand up for righteousness.

Although my mother wasn't a highly educated person and couldn't read, she was wise. When it came to how to raise her children, she was a fountain of wisdom. Not only her words, but her life flowed with insight, especially where her children were concerned. Her intuition was strong, and her vision creative. It was a joy to hear her words each morning because they helped my own life become more abundant. To me, she spoke the mind of God, the heart of which was to show me who I truly am as a daughter of the Almighty.

In the 1960s, Korean villages still didn't have running water or electricity. We studied under oil lamps. As the evenings grew dark, we took an oil lamp with us whenever we went to church.

When I was eight or nine years old, I began helping my mother with heavy chores around the house, such as fetching drinking water. Tasks such as this required a lot of effort, as the water was carried on people's backs.

In summer, households needed mosquito nets if people wanted to get any sleep. I remember how most of the time my siblings and I had to suffer from mosquito attacks during the long summer nights. I would only manage to fall asleep for two or three hours, then it was time to get up and go to school.

In terms of amenities, Korea was far behind most countries. In the village where I lived, there were no televisions. However, once we had electricity, it was possible to own a radio. Our family were the only ones who possessed a radio in our village. People used to gather in our yard to listen to soap operas. They became attached to the storyline, talking amongst themselves about the love life of the characters. They were so emotionally involved that they could hardly wait for the day to end when they could gather around to hear the latest episode. People used to join in singing the songs, like karaoke.

Although most of my neighbors were good people and family-oriented, whenever my mother talked about church and what Jesus meant to her, they weren't at all interested. Many thought my mother must be out of her mind to believe such "nonsense." This didn't faze my mother in the least.

Our fellowship as a family centered around the church, which was eleven miles from our home. Every Sunday we went to church with clean, nicely pressed clothes, our hair washed and combed. We had to look our best for Sunday worship. We were so excited to go to church each week, and we always carried a Bible in our hands. If we didn't have money for our tithes, we took a dozen eggs and some rice instead.

To attend church, we walked each way. My mother carried those of us who couldn't walk such a distance. I held my brother and sisters' hands under the watchful eye of mom. We were a family of faith and, with a few lapses in my younger years, I carry that same dedication to God with me all these years later.

I recall one winter when the snow didn't stop for weeks. It piled up as deep as I was tall. After asking my uncle to shovel the snow and make a path, my mom walked to church anyway. Nothing could stop her from serving God.

At times like this, she wore *komooshin*, shoes made of rubber that reached up to her ankles. The shoes became very slippery in rain or snow. If the snow was heavy enough, she wore a *mahora* (skiff) around her face and neck, along with *basun*, which is a thick kind of sock. Wearing basun, she walked to church without shoes. In the 1960s there were no boots or tennis shoes. Some villagers still wear *jiipshin*, which are handmade rice rips.

My mother was not alone on such occasions; she walked with God on her side. It was dark when she arose for morning prayer, but she wasn't afraid. Her attitude toward life was always positive. She was a disciplined servant of Christ.

A Teenage Rebel

There came a time in my teens when I quite going to church. In my teenage years, I felt lost and began hanging out with the wrong people. They were smokers and spent too much time partying in nightclubs. Though I didn't realize it at the time, I later came to see that they were losers.

Throughout my school years, I wasn't a good student. This caused my mother a lot of problems. I justified this by telling myself I had an eating disorder, a learning disability, and I was defiant. In my teens, I hurt my mom in many ways. I ditched school many days, and spent my time going to the movies, playing pool, or other games in bars. I not only wasn't being the good daughter I should have been, but I was actually losing myself—until the moment I eventually hit rock-bottom.

In those days, I blamed my circumstances on everyone except for myself, complaining about why my life wasn't getting any better when others were doing well and seemed happy. I eventually started to focus on the reason that things weren't going well for me.

As I have recounted, my mother suffered from bronchitis and asthma, which made her life extremely difficult. And here I was, hanging out with the wrong people and spending time chasing after stupid things, like guys whose only interest in me was a one-night stand.

I am not proud of how I acted at this stage in my life. Realizing that my family needed me to work and take my mother to her doctor's appointments, I decided to quit running around with losers, making bad decisions, and staying out late. I realized I had been taking my family and their needs for granted.

My father was gone most of my life, and it was difficult for my mother to raise four children on her own. It was only through her devotion to God that she was able to do what had to be done. I had no idea why my father abused my mother, or why he eventually left. He should have appreciated my mother, as she was completed devoted to both her family and God.

In the worst of my teen years, I couldn't be talked into any particular viewpoint by my mother. However, she continued to teach me simply by the manner in which she lived. As I watched her navigating everyday life, I learned the importance of being humble, as well as the importance of apologizing and asking for forgiveness when wrong.

My mother's ability to show me the way rested in the fact she was a great example of being entirely true to oneself, just as Jesus was true to himself. She was never fake or disloyal to her true nature as a daughter of God. She was at all times the image of sincerity, no matter who she connected with, and this sincerity lasted the whole of her life. Even when she became seriously ill, she never wavered. She was an extremely pure individual, and she lived this way until the day she departed this earthly realm. It was her sincerity that finally touched my heart and brought me back to God.

At heart, I had always sought answers to the big questions of life. Perhaps this stems from the fact that I had become aware of the reality of death at an early age. Our village was on the way to the cemetery, and I remember observing from my room as funerals passed. Three or four times a year we watched from the windows as the long procession winded its way to the graveyard.

Another incident brought death onto the front burner. I was about five years old at the time. An unexpected death occurred in a field not ten minutes from our home. Rumor spread that the individual had been killed by a train, though it was more likely someone had murdered him.

In those days we arose early on Sundays to walk to church. One Sunday morning before sunrise, my mom got up three o'clock and, with an oil lamp, led us by the farm where the dead body was covered with wheat and soil.

Since no one was keen to investigate, by this time the body had been in that spot for two or three months.

Because it wasn't yet dawn, I remember how scared I was walking by the body, even though I held my mother's hand. In that moment, I overheard her pray for the person who killed this soul. The police had been unable to find who had done it. There were three or four potential suspects, but no witnesses, perhaps because it happened in the middle of the night or during a fight. Rumors concerning the perpetrator spread like wildfire in the village, but no one truly seemed to care why the person had been killed.

Thinking about death gave my young mind perspective. It forced me to consider questions such as: *What is death? What's the purpose of life? Why am I here on this earth?* I constantly pondered such issues—not in a negative manner, but with genuine curiosity. I asked my mother questions. Sometimes she would smile knowingly at me, which in itself brought me a sense of comfort.

Not a Dunce After All!

When I graduated from eighth grade, I was required to take a test. We needed to score eighty percent if we wished to be admitted into an elite high school. Each student also needed to talk to the school counselor, who referred them either to the vocational school or the traditional school. The recommendation depended on the student's grades, records, performance in class, and the endorsement of the principle or their key teachers. Since I had failed my courses three or four years in a row, I knew I would be passed up. It was even suggested that I should drop back a few grades. Perhaps this would help me catch up?

I decided I wanted to please my mother. I really didn't care about my prior grades or what my record contained. To please my mother, I asked my counselor to refer me to the traditional school, for which only those students with A or B grades were qualified. The counselor's answer was that this request was impossible.

I decide to talk to my parents and have them consult with the school principal. I was lucky. After my father went to speak with the principal a few times to convince him of my sincerity, the school accepted my request to qualify for the best traditional school, even though I had flunked each semester.

I studied every day for a year and half, seeking to catch up for the three years I was behind in a dozen subjects. As soon as I arose in the mornings, I went directly to school. When school was finished, I went straight to the library to study. Throughout all of this, I kept going to church and Bible study just the same as always.

The winter was cold and there was no heater in the library, so to stay warm I wrapped myself in a blanket from head to toe. I didn't want my feet to get cold, or I might lose my enthusiasm and start skipping my studies.

A few friends studied hard like me, but one day they didn't show up. I learned that they had chosen to hang out on the street with the wrong people. Even though this test was the gateway to the next level of our journey, they didn't seem concerned. In my own case, my conscience convinced me that I had to pay the price if I intended to achieve my goals. No magic pills or miracles could do this for me. Only my love for my mother could motivate me this much. I studied so hard that I experienced several nose bleeds and often didn't sleep at all from the stress. My entire life was directed toward the goal of passing the test.

I recall going with my mother to check the list of those who had passed, as I was confident my name would be on it. As it turned out, I had scored close to one hundred percent, with the exception of math. I actually found most of the test questions to be quite easy. I finished earlier than everyone and walked out proud that I had done a three-year course in the space of one and a half years.

Passing the test meant that I would be admitted to the private Ewha high school. Established during the Lee dynasty over a hundred years ago, it was one of the top private schools in South Korea. My mother, my schoolteacher, and the pastor of our church were thrilled with my achievement.

Most people couldn't believe that I had been accepted into this private women's high school. No one thought I had the determination and persistence to pull it off. For so many years, I had imagined that I was mentally retarded to the point I had actually come to believe it.

Despite my own doubt, my mother continued to believe in me, which is why I found the strength within myself to study and pass the test. I was happy to see my mother's pride in me. Finally, I got the sleep I had been lacking, along with gifts of money from my siblings, cousins, and church members. Passing the test helped in the days ahead when we sought to immigrate. I never ended up going to the school for which I had been accepted because a letter came from the U.S. Embassy allowing us to immigrate.

When we were in Korea, my father worked for the Vietnam Government. Later, he was recruited by the United States to work for the army. Eventually, when I turned fourteen, he decided that we should all immigrate to America.

Ten years had passed since he first went out of our lives, and by now I realized that in addition to forgiving my father, I was ready to receive him back into my life. I could forgive him for the fact that over the years my mother had worked double time to make up for his absence.

Through my mother, God imparted to me a lively imagination.

Looking back today, I liken my journey to a garden. I imagine my journey toward this garden as a rocky, winding, pebbled path that transcends space and time. As I took my first steps along this path, I sensed the small pebbles shift beneath my footfall. I took one step at a time, feeling the tiny rocks as they moved to the left or the right, steadying themselves as I leaned into the next step.

This garden was full of hope—a hope that enveloped my heart and soul. The feeling of comfort as I trod this path was overwhelming, as if I had been here before. Although this was in fact my first visit to the garden, it seemed that every detail had been prepared specifically for me. I knew that in some way, without being able to articulate it, I was no stranger to this path. It was as if I had been dreaming about this place and this time forever.

I realized that I had envisioned this garden countless times, with its beautiful flowers, large and small, in a myriad of colors. Resting close to each other, it was as if each flower had been specially created to coexist exactly where it was.

This perfectly balanced and wonderfully assorted garden, once just a place in my dreams, was now springing to life all around me. I decided there was no place I would rather be. The garden is a place of perfect harmony, synchronicity, and above all, creativity.

I had sensed for many years that the garden would turn out to be everything I dreamed it would be. This beautiful garden was a responsibility that was all my own. I was the one who would pick, prune, and care for each flower.

The garden represents my life, carefully curated as a result of each decision, thought, action, and all the caring and love I could muster. The one thing missing is my father, of his own choice. He is the missing flower from our otherwise perfect garden.

This was a garden in which could create any opportunity. "It will never rain roses," George Eliot once said. "When we want to have more roses, we must plant more seeds." Planting seeds is what my life is all about today.

3

ARRIVING IN THE GARDEN
OF HOPE

An Immigrant's Story

Our time in Korea came to an end in 1977 when we were invited to join my father in America. Before we could arrive in the United States, we had to complete eight to ten rounds of interviews at the United States Embassy.

Obtaining permission to immigrate was a rigorous process, only complicated more by mother's health issues. "We may not be accepted because of my health," my mother revealed one day. Because our education was so important and my father realized that America would offer us the best opportunity, he continued to send us messages asking us not to give up. We eventually passed the entrance interviews and received clearance to immigrate.

I remember arriving at the LAX airport and traveling to the house my father had set up for us. It was close to a library, which made me happy. I loved books and enjoyed reading, so I volunteered at the library, bringing stacks of books home each day.

Life didn't become any easier when we arrived in the U.S. Acclimating to our new environment proved difficult. From the start, we had to attend school as well as work in our family's business.

In high school, I experienced many hardships caused by language and cultural differences. Several people discriminated against our family. Because our home life had instilled a sense of confidence in each of us, we remained proud of who we were. We knew that we were not only loved, but that we were accepted as *individuals*.

Before we arrived, my father had first planted his roots in Maryland and had become a successful entrepreneur and businessman.

He now owned gas stations near where we lived in California and continued to work hard. We would go to his place of work after school and help with the family business. Even though it wasn't an easy life, it seemed like things were moving in the right direction.

Everything was going well until my father walked out on us. My mother was stunned by his irresponsibility toward the family. Our life went from hard to seemingly impossible.

I had to make my own adjustments to a very different culture, so I didn't have the energy or the time to emotionally deal with the impact of my father's departure. In Korean culture, it isn't a redeeming quality to be a middle child. In fact, I always felt different from other children. But now my mother, brothers, and sisters needed me to make money, and I had no choice but to drop out of high school and work to support the family. If I didn't work, we wouldn't eat.

To be honest, I wasn't all that disappointed to quit school. I hated it and found it boring. It didn't help that I had grown up thinking of myself as having learning disabilities, despite proving otherwise before we left Korea. It was just a matter of not being interested in the lessons that were taught.

I continued to work, at one point having three different cashier jobs simultaneously. When the wolf is at the door, one takes whatever work one can get, always bearing in mind that it's just a temporary steppingstone. I was happy to do what I had to do for my family. I loved them dearly and was willing to assist in any way I could.

My mother spent most of her time focusing on my brother. He was one year older than me, and eventually decided he couldn't take one more day of life. At the young ago of thirty-four, he left this planet, bringing great sadness to the whole family. His death was particularly devastating for my mother and myself. I loved him dearly, and his departure was a tragedy.

My brother and I grew up together. He was the best brother ever.

To this day, I feel sorry that I didn't detect what was happening in his inner world. His departure left me grief stricken, especially since I was unable to be there for him in the way he needed. I know he tried. He didn't really wish to end his life in this way. My mother was particularly surprised that he left his wife and two children to fend for themselves, which was so unlike him. One never knows what another person may be suffering internally.

A part of me eventually started to look for an escape from my circumstances, because this was easier than dealing head-on with the situation. However, as the condition of my mother worsened, I realized I needed to shift my perspective. As I was her daughter, I realized it was my responsibility to take care of her. I began to change my attitude and refocus my attention to her needs.

To support my mother, I began to focus on not being controlled by my circumstances. I wanted my mother to live as comfortably and as healthy of a life as she possibly could. I treated her as if she was a beautiful flower in my garden of life, constantly nurturing her and providing all that she needed.

Forgiving the Unforgivable

As time passed, I realized that this time my father was gone for good, having given us no sense of why he had abandoned us. At first, I prayed for his return and was prepared to forgive him for leaving us without support. We needed his strength, and he could not be replaced.

When my father left us the first time, back in Korea, I was challenged to follow my mother's example by forgiving him for his mistreatment of her and for leaving us for so long. However, following the beating I witnessed him give to my mother, I could never bring myself to respect him, let alone like him. I had also learned that in the past my mother had been forced to flee to my grandmother's house during those moments when she could no longer stand my father's abuse. My uncle was always the one who pushed her to return home.

But this time when my father left, I knew I should forgive him just as my mother had done.

When I realized that forgiving his irresponsible actions was more difficult that I thought, I prayed for the ability to do so. I didn't find forgiveness easily. It took me a long time to let go of the memory of the night he attacked my mother, but I was eventually able to do so. I knew this was the right thing to do. My mother taught me that if I wanted to move on with my journey, forgiveness was the only way to do so.

I respect my mother's words of wisdom. She recognized that my father was doing the best he could. In the end, from God's point of view, there is no simple way of dividing things into right or wrong.

Everything that happens in our life is a lesson. Life is a great educator in so many ways.

From the time my father first left us in Korea, it took me a fifty years to truly let go of the heavy weight he placed on my heart. I told myself that Jesus Christ died for all of us, including my father. When I was finally able to take the step of forgiving him, I know it pleased my mother. I felt so free releasing the burden I had carried all these decades.

I practice forgiveness regularly today because it releases the kind of thinking that harms not only myself, but also those I care about. I don't harbor negative thoughts because all they do is smother the good seeds I have planted in my garden. Life is full of generosity, so showing gratitude and compassion toward others is now my purpose in life. Forgiveness touches the heart of who we are; by forgiving others, we seek to be the best versions of ourselves.

There is a reason that forgiveness is the core of the Christian faith. I will never forget a lesson my mother taught me when we were in Korea. One day we talked to Pastor Park who told my mother that she would not betray her husband if she stopped praying for him. "He has done nothing to seek forgiveness," the pastor assured her.

You would think the pastor's words would cause my mother to give up on my father. On the contrary, she never stopped praying for him. When we were in Korea, as I recounted above, she even asked him to return home. After ten years of absence, her hopes eventually came to fruition and worked for our good, leading to our immigration to the United States. I learned from my mother that when we forego resentment and are gracious to others despite their limitations, we benefit not just the individual but also ourselves.

Korean Style Traditional House

Kicked Out of House and Home

My mother's unwillingness to judge, as well as her endlessly forgiving spirit, came through in other ways. When my father brought other women to live with us, she allowed them to use the family bedroom. She didn't judge their actions, realizing that each must take their own path in life.

Isn't this the lesson of the parable of the Prodigal Son? When the lad asked his father for his inheritance, the father willingly gave it to him, even though this was an insult to the aging patriarch. When the son had squandered the money away and lost his friends, he came home to ask if he could work as a servant. The father wouldn't hear of such a thing, instead treating him like royalty. The father sent for a ring, fresh shoes, and a change of clothing so that no one in the village would know his son had been sleeping among the pigs. Then he ordered the servants to prepare a feast.

My mother did the same for my father's girlfriends, getting the room ready for them by providing clean bedsheets and a new blanket while my mother and us children moved into what was more like a hut. One day my father told her to leave, which meant abandoning her children to his girlfriend. She had no option but to do as he said. He kicked her out of her own house!

My mother worked at a factory and was once gone for six months. Leaving her three children behind was devastating to her. Why had God allowed someone else to take her position in the family, stealing her husband, her children, and her own bedroom, which was her prayer room? Still, she prayed for each of them.

Eventually, my father began looking for her and invited her to come home. The house was in chaos without her, as were the lives of her children. Nothing was the way she left it. His girlfriend had run off with most of what we possessed, but at least my mother's prayers had been answered and she was back in our lives.

We decided to hold a Bible study with a party to celebrate her return. My mother prepared the best food for this Bible study. Going to markets, she bought fresh fish, meat, vegetables, and side dishes, as well as a bag of cookies and candies. It took her two days to prepare the food. To do so was a delight to her, despite her increasingly ailing health. With joy in my heart, I watched as she praised the Lord while cooking.

After the Bible study, the dining table was piled with delicious food for the pastor and our guests. I remember waiting for the final prayer so I could get a chunk of my favorite rainbow star candy. I sat in my mom's lap observing the festivities.

My mother also continued to pray for those siblings who had betrayed her in the past. Her dedication was second to none. Even though she was sick, she never ceased praying. At times she would fast for an entire week to focus on the Lord, which showed tremendous self-discipline. She was truly a most beautiful human being, and her sincerity shone out of her each and every day.

A Mother's Example Makes All the Difference

My mother was the most disciplined human being I have ever known. As I grew a little older, she showed me respect as an independent person, not as a copy of herself. She didn't just accept me, she helped me to correct my mistakes in the most gracious way.

Through her daily teaching and example, she helped me inculcate the core Christian values of life. This has enabled me to use each day to gradually become a more Christ-like individual.

Through my mother's example, I learned the importance of serving others before thinking of myself—not by denying who I am or my own needs, but as an extension of the nature of Christ within me. I saw how Jesus' self-denial was a fulfillment of his true nature, not a denigration of himself.

For this reason, I now sow seeds of kindness wherever I happen to be. Practicing forgiveness helps us banish fear from our lives, as doing so teaches us the worth of all humans. I seek to be a person whose life overflows with generosity, regardless of what someone may have done. When we understand a person and forgive them, it doesn't excuse what they did; on the contrary, it encourages them to look deeper into themselves, which may help them realize that they are also a child of God.

If there's something I can't easily forgive, I pray about it. This removes the blockage, allowing divine love to flow toward the person. I remind myself how much of God's goodness has been shared with me, especially through my mother. She showed me that there is no one who is beyond the pale of forgiveness, not even my father.

About six years before my mother's death, her best friend suddenly passed away. A prayer warrior like my mother, Mrs. Jung was ten years her senior. My mother was shocked by her friend's sudden death because it was unexpected. As spiritual companions, they spent a great deal of time together. You might say they were soulmates. When I wasn't around, Mrs. Jung was my mother's "bodyguard."

Upon hearing of her friend's death, my mother was devastated and wept. But then she rose to the challenge, mastering herself. She thanked God for taking her friend to Heaven where she could now rest in eternal peace.

Mrs. Jung had an interesting life of her own. She escaped from North Korea during the Korean war. She had lost her husband and two of her children during the flight south. She and the three surviving children almost died too. Landing in South Korea, she did everything she could to provide for her children, making sure they were well educated. In time, she also immigrated to the United States, which is how she and my mother became prayer warriors together.

All of us need a purpose in life, and I find that I am no exception.

As I sought to discover my purpose, I decided to take each day a few pebbles at a time. Traversing the path of life, I focused on those pebbles that were under my feet each during each step of the journey. I noticed the pebbles left behind me, fully experienced the pebbles under my feet, and moved forward in the direction of the pebbles that lay ahead of me.

We should all live our lives one pebble at a time, taking the good with the bad, the small pebbles with the large, the smooth ones with the rough ones. Each pebble is unique in its own existence, an illustration of how life's many experiences are each special in their own way.

Every pebble is an invitation to learn to live in a more abundant manner. The pebbles slowly teach us how to *be*. The journey to the garden is created and sculpted by the pebbles we encounter along the path.

For the period when my mother was moving toward the end of her life here on earth, a profound sense came over me that I had been born with the task of protecting my mother at this time. These were the pebbles that life had placed under my feet. She was my reason for being here at this time. I derived a sense of purpose from watching over her by day and night.

I believe that children choose their parents, so that the family into which we are born is no accident. I am the offspring of a mother that I was proud of, and I'm so grateful that we chose each other. I am delighted to have been my mother's child.

Knowing how proud I was of her, my mother also cautioned us when it came time for her death. She didn't want us idolizing her in any way. In her last will, she instructed us not to bow when we come to see her, and not to bring food and candles to her grave. She wanted her children to honor her, but not worship her. It was important to her that we had no idols and that we worshiped only God and his son Jesus.

A Model of Spiritual Steadfastness

Despite how sick my mother eventually became, she had succeeded in raising my three siblings and myself. She was the core of our Christian family, leaving us a legacy that would span generations to come.

Our lives were moving one pebble at a time toward my mother's departure. After screening her chest with x-rays, the doctor admitted, "I haven't seen a chest like this before. I don't know how your mother is able to breathe, let alone carry on with her life. Her chest is half full of water that has strange dust particles in it with the appearance of smoke. I can understand why she is in terrible pain."

I confess that I was devastated by what the doctor said. I explained how my mother worked in a dusty clothing factory when she was young. Nevertheless, I continued to search for other doctors who might be able to help restore my mother to health. I made it my mission in life. In the end I took her to three other doctors, each time without success.

As my mother's bronchitis and asthma worsened, the doctor at the UCLA hospital recommended she should have an oxygen tank that should be carried with her at all times. The additional oxygen would support her chest pain and improve her breathing.

No matter how sick my mother was, she never missed a single day of prayer. The oxygen tube was in her mouth, but the Bible was in her hand. She always cleaned herself up, donning her best dress before beginning to pray. She was God's daughter, and she wanted to look her best for her heavenly Father.

Her prayer always started with praising the Lord, thanking her heavenly Father for his graciousness. Her prayer then focused on forgiveness and the cleansing blood of Jesus Christ. She called out the names of each person who was in her mind, blessing each of them and sending love to them in the name of Christ. Her prayers moved to the leaders of various nations, including South Korean and North Korea. Finally, she prayed for prosperity and abundance for the entire global family.

In the months that followed, I did my best to comfort her, taking her to the hospital regularly for checkups. We are only fortunate to ever have one mother, and she can never be replaced. I wanted her to be happy, with all her needs fulfilled. Whatever I was able to do for her, I put my whole heart into it.

Even though I did my best to serve my mother, I wanted to ask God why her life was one of such hardship. It didn't seem fair. I loved my mother and wanted to spend as much time with her as possible. I cherished our time together, while also recognizing that she was sick and not getting any better. Taking care of her was my greatest pleasure, but it also left me feeling sad for her, not to mention stressed at times.

While I slept, my subconscious knew how to guard my mother. It was important to me that she was comfortable at all times, and I didn't let anyone or anything disturbing her comfort if it could be helped.

"It's in God's Hands Now"

When a person's death is near, doctors are apt to say, "We've done all we can. It's in God's hands now."

As I think about this, I realize that every step of the way was always in God's hands. We might not understand the reason for things at the time, and perhaps never in this life, but throughout our lives there is plenty of evidence that we are guided by His spirit. I do not know why my mother had to suffer so much, but I know that she learned to live abundantly, peacefully, and joyously despite all that befell her. I learned a life-changing lesson from this, as did many who were close to her.

Knowing that taking care of my mother was my purpose in life at this time, whatever she was doing automatically became a part of my life. I was an extension of her soul and flesh. Whenever I looked into her eyes and saw her happy face, it made my day. Whenever I noticed that she was in pain and had a worried appearance, her pain became my pain.

The day came when I turned twenty-eight years old and planned to get married. Today, I am thankful to have two children, Grace and David. However, my love for my mother remains as strong as ever. Even today, I love her so much.

To see me marry was a delight for my mother, but at my wedding I noticed she was weeping. Although it was time for me to set up my own home, I was well aware that she still needed me. After the wedding, I told her, "Mom, even though I'm married, I don't intend to leave you. I plan to live with you even though I'm married."

The pain my mother had to go through was so terrible that I prayed for God to let me suffer it instead of her. I hated for her to be sick and wished I could take her burden on myself. No matter how sick she was, my mother always had a kind smile for everyone.

During one of her regular checkups, the doctor informed me that they had found an ovarian tumor, advising me that she should be treated with either surgery or ten rounds of chemotherapy. I was shocked and scared. How would my mother survive chemotherapy when she couldn't breathe without her oxygen tank? As the therapy got underway and it became evident that the chemo itself was hastening her death, I prayed fervently that God would assist her body in ridding itself of the tumor.

After each dose of chemo, my mother resembled a dead frog. I would give her a massage and stay with her, praying with her. All night long, she coughed and coughed. Even though I put all my strength into supporting her, at times I really didn't know how to help. I hated feeling powerless. The realization that there was only so much I could do to ease her pain weighed heavily on me. Today I comfort myself by realizing I did my best.

Despite the ten treatments of chemotherapy, my mother's tumor persisted. The doctor raised her oxygen tank levels to maximum, helping her breathe more comfortably. I was devastated when he told us to be prepared for her death.

Most of my mother's hair had disappeared as a result of the chemotherapy. At times she appeared to be in a vegetative state. We were clearly approaching the end of her time on earth. Her breathing was becoming shorter and she couldn't sleep. We prepared ourselves for the end, knowing that she would soon rest in peace. I didn't want to let her go.

The day came when my mother wasn't moving, even though her oxygen tank was connected. I tried to talk to her. "Mom, are you okay?" I touched her body gently to check her pulse. I was so sacred she had passed away. Death was knocking on her door. The day came when the doctor confirmed to the nurse who tended her, "She's at rest now. We can take away the breathing machine."

I couldn't believe that my mother was no longer on this planet with me. I didn't think I could live without her. At the funeral,

I cried so much that I felt faint. I thought of the life she had lived—the abuse, the betrayal, and all the resentment she had to overcome. She had birthed seven children. She did this despite how weak and sick she was. She was born June 1, 1936. Her life was devoted to God until she finally passed at the age of sixty-five.

I ask myself why my mother had to go through this terrible sickness, when all she deserved was health and happiness. She was a messenger of God, and I wanted to better understand why He wasn't taking care of her the way I thought He should. I wasn't upset, but I wanted answers because I loved her so deeply.

Even though twenty years have passed since my mother left us, I am grateful for who I am today because of the path that she guided me along. There were times when it wasn't easy to break through to what I wanted to achieve, but with her help I was always able to figure my way around the obstacles in my life.

Getting in Tune with the Laws of the Universe

So here I was, an immigrant living in America with very little direction. I felt confused and out of place. I wasn't sure how my life was supposed to fit into this changing environment.

My mother's death eventually led to me ask some questions: How do I honor my birth? How can I make my life truly worthwhile? How do I express myself on this earthly plane? Who are the significant people in my life? Am I truly serving others with loving care? What legacy will I leave behind me?

In the weeks that followed my mother's departure from this earthly presence, all that her life had taught me began to well up inside me. As a result, today I choose to live the abundant kind of life that my mother aspired to instill in me.

My promise to my mother is to create a life worthy of her. I know this was her will for me, because she wished this for everyone whose life she touched—even my father. She longed for everyone to create a life that has godly meaning. I know of no one quite like her.

My aim is to express the soul of my being in everyday life. How can I best express what I stand for? What dreams do I wish to impart upon those whose lives I touch? What does it mean to serve people with the kind of integrity exemplified by my mother? These are the questions I ask myself as I go about my everyday duties.

There came a point when I made a decision concerning how I would live. I decided to seek out the truth embedded in the laws of the universe. As I did so, everything my mother taught me bubbled to the surface.

I discovered that there is a law of universal energy, and our energy is fed by our intentions. The key to growing our faith is to take baby steps each and every day. If my dream is to climb Mount Everest, I can only do so by putting one foot in front of the other, one step at a time.

Little by little a dream began to emerge and find its feet. I was learning that if my intention was fully focused on what I feel inspired to do, nothing I dream of is beyond the range of possibility.

When we feed our faith, it makes our days more alive. This is the secret of true freedom. Today, I see the importance of giving my full attention to the possibilities that life shows me. New possibilities come our way each and every day. I am more determined than ever not to sabotage the opportunities life sends my way. I know now what a precious gift life is.

Today I enjoy living in the freedom my mother passed on to me.

The way the universe works is that everything we have and are has been gifted to us. It comes to us and costs us nothing. In my case, my mind emanates from my mother, as do my emotions and my physical makeup. I can never repay all that has been bequeathed to me; I can only pay it forward.

This I do by paying attention to my dreams, then figuring out how to make them reality. I'm speaking of those dreams that inspire meaningful relationships that are the opposite of what I experienced at times with my family in Korea.

I am interested in making this a better world, a world in which we serve one another by being true to the person God made us to be. We are all given possibilities that enable us to serve one another in ways that suite who we are intrinsically. We need to identify those ways of serving that are most suitable to each of us. God never asks us to be someone different from the unique person He created us to be.

I am presently involved in consciously building my life—a life I love to live as I serve people. I have learned that when God wishes to create something through us, it always starts within us, so that we create from the inside out.

Planting Good Seeds

Another law of the universe says that planting good seeds is all that is necessary for the bad seeds to perish. By making space in our mind for the good seeds to flourish, we nourish a healthy mindset. Each of us has been entrusted with an abundance of good seeds from which we are able to create a lush garden.

When we succumb to doubt, we actually undermine our God-given dreams. Even the smallest amount of doubt can choke our dreams by causing us to be afraid of following up on our intentions. I learned that we choose the things we think about. It's crucial that we guard our minds, because where we place our intention is extremely important. It serves us well to plant only thoughts of abundance.

Entrepreneurship thrives when there is freedom of speech, science, and the belief that no authority is higher than any other. Today, I expect abundance and prosperity in every part of my life. Even when someone shows up who threatens my happiness, I am still able to be joyful because these are the pebbles that life has placed under my feet at that moment for a specific purpose.

My mother was an advanced person who understood that she could exercise a degree of mastery over her life. She could not change what happened to her health early in life, but she could determine how she responded to each situation she was in. No obstacle could stop her from seeing God in every aspect of her life. I have learned that it's from the presence of the obstacles in my own life that I am able to harness more of the divine nature at my core—the divine nature revealed in Jesus.

Difficult people and events always end up expanding us. They teach us to let things go and let God take over *through* us. Any thoughts of resentment that arise in us, we can then quickly let pass by wishing the person well, which releases us to experience only the good.

This is my approach to any situation that presents itself in my life. I have found that it's important not to wallow in thoughts of scarcity, regardless of what's happening on the physical plane.

The entire universe tends toward good. When we are attuned to spirit, it empowers us to see good everywhere. It doesn't matter how humble our birth was. Spirit can use any circumstance to mold us into the divine image revealed in Jesus. By enlivening our thoughts, it transforms any and all circumstances for our good, as long as we continue to feed our faith.

We may not immediately see what a situation portends, but faith enables us to move forward, nevertheless. Spirit imparts to each of us wisdom as we need it, bringing us the clarity that changes everything—one pebble at a time.

I am living my dreams—dreams implanted in my soul by my mother. There is no right or wrong way to live, but I choose to live in the fashion my mother taught me. Her vision inspires me even now. I want my life to be one in which I inspire others to design their own lives according to the laws of serving, giving, kindness, sincerity, integrity, honesty, and sacrifice.

To be able to breathe with the great spirit of life given to me by my mother is part of the universe's desire to foster cooperation among all creatures. Cooperation is the preeminent law of the universe.

In my imagination—in my own secret world—I fly with my mother behind me, her arms around my shoulders holding onto me. I fly with her to Heaven and live with her there. I comfort my mother and we live happily and peacefully forever.

4

DISCOVERING MY CALLING

A New Purpose Reveals Itself

"I can control my destiny, but not my fate," said the author of *The Alchemist,* Paulo Coelho. "Destiny means there are opportunities to turn right or left, but fate is a one-way street. I believe we all have the choice as to whether we fulfill our destiny, but our fate is sealed."

So far in this book I have described aspects of my destiny that paved the way for me to discover my fate, or what I refer to as my "calling." Sometimes, when we look back, a pattern emerges that can only be identified in hindsight. In the end, we realize that everything has been leading to what it is we are on earth to accomplish—our calling.

Post-World War II, substantial changes were occurring back in Korea, and it was no longer safe for us to live there. Just after I turned fourteen, a series of decisions brought me to this beautiful country of America. I said earlier that moving to America from a small village in South Korea came with a lot of culture shock. The huge transition involved proved to be worth it, as the poverty of

South Korea yielded to the great opportunities that awaited us in the United States.

During the beginning of the Vietnam War, my father's job was to assist American soldiers in understanding the Korean language. His job as a translator for the U.S. Army was clearly used to open up this different life for me.

As a Christian family, my mother had worked hard to raise each of us with strong character and high morals. Here in the U.S., my mother continued the same practice of offering help to those in need. Making every person she came across feel as if they were the most important person in the world was her gift, and her generosity trickled down to her children.

Faith was an important part of our lives. Going all the way back to our early days of childhood, when we weren't yet able to truly understand to whom we prayed, we knew how crucial it was to maintain a strong faith. We respected the wishes of our mother, following her lead.

As my siblings grew, faith became an important part of our lives and our relationship with the world around us.

As I entered my adult years, I was involved with a number of different jobs. All of this led to my purpose being revealed; it came to me in the strangest of ways.

A Reason for Being Here

I was a real estate agent on the day I met my calling. If I simply close my eyes, I can still paint a vivid picture of this period of my life. It's ingrained in my mind, and I will never forget the fateful car journey when the calling became clear to me.

My closest friend owned a rickety car, and it was always breaking down. So, it was no surprise when he called me on a warm California day asking that I give him a ride to see a friend. I agreed to pick him up, and he asked me to take him to a small school in Compton, California.

He had told me of this school on numerous occasions. He also indicated he thought I should consider meeting the head of the school. My friend went on and on about the school, offering me detail after detail, indicating that he thought it would be a great place for me to work.

I had never once thought of entering the educational realm, so I considered his suggestion to be quite silly. As we drove the thirty or so miles to Compton, joking with one another as most friends do, little did I know that my calling was about to emerge.

When we eventually pulled into the driveway of the school, my intention was to have my friend hop out, while I drove on to the real estate listings I had scheduled.

As we pulled in, he insisted I survey the quant little university. Begrudgingly, I agreed to do so.

As I exited the vehicle, he grabbed my hand and said, "This is the university you will be working at!" I laughed at this weird remark, then followed him up the driveway.

As I approached the entrance, I saw a large red and white sign with the name "Yuin University" emblazoned in a deep red color. A short mission statement was etched under the name. It read: "At Yuin University, out students not only learn to find success, they learn how to give their lives meaning—in the classroom, studying abroad, or through volunteer work. It's all about getting the most from your college experience—so you can get the most of life."

For whatever reason, I smiled as I read this statement. Yuin seemed like a nice college, but not one I had anything but a passing interest in.

As we made our way to the entrance of the university, we were greeted by a middle-aged woman who exuded great energy. My friend immediately introduced me. "This is Christine," he began. "She is going to work at your school."

I couldn't believe my ears. At first, I thought this was some kind of joke. However, the woman's response wasn't indicative of a joke. She appeared to be completely serious. "Christine, thank you so much for coming," she said as my friend retreated into the building, leaving me alone with this woman. "Your friend has told me so much about you. I know this may seem crazy to you, but I would like to give you the keys to this school. I need help, and your friend has told me he thinks you can run my school."

"Thank you so much," I said, feeling confused. "But I do not want to work at a school, and I certainly don't want to run one. I have no experience in education, or for that matter, running much of anything. I am not even looking for a job. This is all very strange. It's so kind of you to offer me this opportunity, but this is not for me."

"I have run this school for many years," the woman replied. "This is not for me anymore either. I am aging, and these days I easily become tired. The job calls for someone with energy to take charge, and I suspect you have both of these qualities. We have almost $35,000 in our operating account to run the programs.

Dozens of students are enrolled, so more tuition money will be coming in."

The woman reached into her pocket and pulled out a single key. She took my wrist, opened my hand, and placed the single silver key in my palm while holding my wrist. Even though I was much younger, for some reason I wasn't able to pull away. She closed my hand, and I clenched my fist.

We both looked down, and then back up as our eyes met. Suddenly I felt drawn to this woman. When she asked me to come back a few days later, on February 12, 2012, I knew I was meant to take over her position as head of the school.

I felt like I had been hit by a tidal wave! I stood there, dumbfounded and speechless.

In the days that followed, I went back and forth between excitement and sheer fear. It seemed like a wonderful opportunity, but who starts their day as a real estate agent and ends up as head of a university?

I said to myself, *The real estate business is slow right now, and for whatever reason I feel drawn to this school.* Besides, education meant so much to my family, and I knew my mother would be proud to see me take charge. I decided to jump right in. I told myself, *I'll only do it for a year or so.*

My mother taught me to be flexible. She told me that the key to a great life is to live in such a way that we are able to cope when life sends unexpected twists and turns our way. She wanted me to be prepared to incorporate changes into my life whenever necessary. There are times when the world needs us to change, and we shouldn't be afraid of this but should follow the principles the Scripture teaches.

My Work Was Cut Out for Me

As I began my work at the school, I realized there were many problems with the small university. The staff were pleasant and the students enjoyed the learning process, but we were receiving regular correspondence from Consumer Affairs, the governing body of the university.

The bureau exists to promote and protect the interests of students and consumers: (i) through the effective and efficient oversight of California's private postsecondary educational institutions, (ii) through the promotion of competition that rewards educational quality and employment outcomes, (iii) through proactively combating unlicensed activity, and (iv) by resolving student complaints in a manner that benefits both the complaining student and future students.

One might think the governing body would act as our ally, but I came to understand there was a substantial amount of tension between our faculty and Consumer Affairs. I did everything needed to ensure the university followed the rules and regulations outlined by Consumer Affairs. I registered Yuin University and ensured I had all the necessary paperwork in place.

There was a great mess to clean up, and the letters from Consumer Affairs continued to pour in. I learned that they were challenging our accreditation, which presented a substantial problem for us. Without accreditation, we could no longer operate as a university and would be forced to shut down. Although I had just started my job, I decided to fight to keep the university open. I couldn't quite explain why, but I felt deeply connected to Yuin and all the wonderful opportunities we offered to students.

As I approached the mailbox each day, I became more and more wary of correspondence from Consumer Affairs. With each passing letter, it appeared we were edging inches closer to having no choice but to shut down. It almost felt as if there was a target on our back, and Consumer Affairs was firing warning shot after warning shot, getting closer and closer to hitting the bullseye.

Each time I opened the mailbox, my heart sank as I saw yet another letter with Consumer Affairs' emblem on the envelope. I rifled through the rest of the mail and quickly tore open the letter. It was my worst nightmare. The letter indicated that Yuin University would have no choice but to close down on March 15, 2013. A Consumer Affairs attorney wrote the letter, and it indicated that I would be sued and that they and file an emergency injunction if I chose not to cooperate with their demands.

I couldn't believe it. I was falling in love with the school. I had come to truly enjoy awaking and driving to the university, greeting the students, and closely working with the faculty to implement new curriculum. Now the authorities wanted to take this away from me.

I wasn't a lawyer, so I didn't understand why they would close the school. Their problem was with the previous owner. I had nothing to do with his issues, yet the state decided to take their anger out on me. I learned that the previous owner had quite the negative reputation with Consumer Affairs and faced thirty-one different violations during his time as owner and headmaster. Now I would have to pay for his mistakes.

I thought of my options, and ultimately decided not to close the school. They'd have to come put the lock on the door themselves. It took me numerous lawyers and tens of thousands of dollars before I found an attorney willing to fight for me. We began reviewing the case together, and through our correspondence with Consumer Affairs, I learned that they believed the previous management was a fraud. They thought the university was selling the promise of degrees, but had only issued less than ten legitimate degrees since its inception. The accusations were substantial, and the case appeared to be daunting—so much so that my lawyer recommended I settle with the state and move onto something else.

I hadn't wanted the job in the first place, but now that I was in charge, I couldn't let them take this opportunity away. I just couldn't quit. This was my calling. I had made the choice to take on the school and had to deliver on my promise.

I argued continuously with my lawyer, who thought I was an idiot for fighting. He didn't see a path to victory, only certain defeat.

Nevertheless, I decided to fight, and he agreed to fight for me—even though I knew he did so only for the money. I knew I did nothing wrong and ran an honest and morally sound program. From day one, I instilled in Yuin the character my mother instilled in me.

The trial was set to begin in October 2015. I was nervous, although I always felt a sense of calmness throughout the process itself. On the first day of the trial, I admitted to my lawyer how scared I was. He told me I could still throw in the towel, but I declined. For purposes of scheduling, the case was reset to March 2016.

When the trial finally began, Consumer Affairs called a number of witnesses against Yuin University. They detailed their allegations to the judge, outlining the specific violations one after the other.

I was in complete shock. I couldn't believe how real it all was.

Then I remembered the words of my mother, "God will watch over you from the front, not the back." What did these words mean in my present situation? Whatever they meant, they kept me strong through the weeks-long trial.

My Mentor Sets Me Straight

During one of the shorter breaks, I met my mentor Bob Proctor at a coffee shop in Los Angeles. As I sat sipping coffee, Bob enjoyed a sandwich. He inquired about the trial. I must have sounded hysterical. Through my tears I told him, "I think the university will close down. No one is helping me. My lawyer is more scared than I am. What do I do?"

Bob said nothing. He just continued eating.

I knew from my mother that if we anticipate that life will present us with problems and aren't rattled when it does, there's no need to rush around seeking a solution when an issue rears its head. Instead, we know that the wise course is to stay calm, trusting that the answer will present itself to us intuitively. We pray, sleep on it, and allow the solution to emerge. This way, we discover that every problem also offers us an opportunity. No problem is ever the end of the world.

Bob knew this, as did my mother. This is why he simply continued eating until the solution sprang into his awareness. He was accustomed to waiting for his intuition to kick in before answering a question. I had yet to put this final brick in place when it came to following my own intuition. The situation I found myself in had come into my life for this very purpose.

"Bob, I'm all alone," I pleaded. "No one is listening to me. I have nothing but my school. I gave up my career for this. Next Monday will probably be my last day. They will close me down. Are you even listening to me? Bob? *Bob?*"

He remained silent.

"Bob, are you understanding what I'm telling you? Do you realize that my school is closing down? Is there any advice you can give me? What should I do?"

Finally, Bob finished his sandwich and looked up at me. Smiling, he said, "Christine, write down what you want."

That's it. After all I had shared with him, this was his reply.

I responded, "What do you mean, 'Write down what I want'? I can't just write this down. What are you talking about?"

He looked at me again and said, "Just write it down."

"All I want is for the school to remain open. I want Consumer Affairs to leave me alone and let me run my school. That's it."

"Then write it down," Bob said. "Don't forget to also write down the things that you are happy and grateful for. And put a 'thank you' at the end."

He continued, "Once you write it down, you'll be surprised how you can turn your entire universe around. Write it down 3,000 times."

I almost burst into laughter. This was his solution?

The trial was set to begin again in just three days. How could I write this down 3,000 times in three days? I decided I would at least try. I looked at Bob and smiled, thinking to myself, *How can this possibly work?*

I left the coffee shop and went directly to Yuin. I walked into my office and wrote the following:

I am so happy for the school remain open. I am so happy that the litigation is over, and I am the new owner. I am so happy I can provide these wonderful students with an education.

Over the next three days, I spent almost every waking minute writing down that statement. I thought my hand would fall off. With the last repetition, I took the small piece of paper, folded it, and placed it in the pocket of the jacket I would wear in court. Could Bob possibly be right?

My trial started again the following day. More witnesses. More testimony. More of the same. I was still scared, but I put my hand in my jacket pocket and rubbed that folded piece of paper. As the day ended, my lawyer confronted me and said, "Christine, I'm just letting you know that if we don't show up tomorrow, you'll be okay. You'll be out of everything. You don't even have to be here. We can pay the fines, and you can close the school. One day, you can open a new one. It will be okay."

I refused to listen. This was my calling. I told my lawyer I would most definitely show up. I asked that he sit beside me and have faith. "God will cause me to win," I assured him. He even had the nerve to call me an idiot, again!

As we appeared in court the following day, we took our places and awaited the judge. He took the bench and asked that both my lawyer and the lawyers from Consumer Affairs to approach. I could tell by his facial expressions that he was upset. How much more could I handle? Motioning for the lawyers to return back to their respective desks, he said the following:

"This case has no merits. Consumer Affairs has no case here. You are suing the wrong person. She did not commit these violations."

He continued on, "Where is the individual who actually committed the violations? Why didn't you bring him to court? Why would you waste the court's time with this nonsense? This case is over. I am dismissing the allegations and closing this matter. Yuin University can continue to operate so long as Ms. Lee is the new owner and has no ties to previous management.

And just like that, it was done. Bob was right. I was right. My faith was right. My choices were right.

As of the publishing of this book, Yuin University is enjoying close to full capacity and regularly graduating students with post-secondary degrees. It has become an environment for learning and cultural development. I am proud that I didn't give up. I am grateful that I didn't succumb to the fear I felt. It wasn't always easy, but mentors and support appeared when I needed them most.

While I know that much of what occurred was because of my intuitive choices, which sometimes went against all reasoning, I cannot help but think that it was my mother and her faith that guided me. It always seemed like an unexplained force was preparing my path, one pebble at a time.

Above all, the victory that was handed to me required me to believe in my intuition. The steps I took were so often an act of pure faith.

I am grateful for the wisdom to follow my intuition as it inspired me to close my hand around that key. This one event allowed me to work diligently as an educator, shaping the destinies of so many students each and every day.

Who would have thought that an F student could rise to become owner of a university? Such is the power of dedication to God and following one's God-given intuition.

TO MY MOTHER

Mother, even though you left this planet twenty-five years ago, I wanted to let you know how much I dearly love you. It's an honor for me to write this love letter. I have dreamed about doing this for many years. My dreams have now come true and I am sending big love to you. I miss you! You are the best educator and teacher ever, and I am so grateful to have been raised by you.

MY MOTHER'S FAVORITE SCRIPTURES

These verses still sound in my ears. Even though my mother couldn't read the Bible for herself, since she could neither read nor write, she listened to passages of the Bible through recordings, which is how I know what some of her favorite texts were. I could almost be there in our family home listening to them, they were such a part of our lives.

Psalm 28

My mother loved this psalm because it calls on God to defend us against all who intend evil against us.

> *{A Psalm of David.} Unto thee will I cry, O LORD my rock; be not silent to me: lest, if thou be silent to me, I become like them that go down into the pit. Hear the voice of my supplications, when I cry unto thee, when I lift up my hands toward thy holy oracle.*
>
> *Draw me not away with the wicked, and with the workers of iniquity, which speak peace to their neighbours, but mischief is in their hearts.*
>
> *Give them according to their deeds, and according to the wickedness of their endeavours: give them after the work of*

their hands; render to them their desert. Because they regard not the works of the LORD, nor the operation of his hands, he shall destroy them, and not build them up.

Blessed be the LORD, because he hath heard the voice of my supplications.

The LORD is my strength and my shield; my heart trusted in him, and I am helped: therefore my heart greatly rejoiceth; and with my song will I praise him.

The LORD is their strength, and he is the saving strength of his anointed. Save thy people, and bless thine inheritance: feed them also, and lift them up for ever.

Psalm 34

This was a favorite of my mother because it shows how God prepares our path before us.

I will bless the Lord at all times: his praise shall continually be in my mouth. My soul shall make her boast in the Lord: the humble shall hear thereof, and be glad. O magnify the Lord with me, and let us exalt his name together. I sought the Lord, and he heard me, and delivered me from all my fears. They looked unto him, and were lightened: and their faces were not ashamed. This poor man cried, and the Lord heard him, and saved him out of all his troubles. The angel of the Lord encampeth round about them that fear him, and delivereth them. O taste and see that the Lord is good: blessed is the man that trusteth in him. O fear the Lord, ye his saints: for there is no want to them that fear him. The young lions do lack, and suffer hunger: but they that seek the Lord shall not want any good thing. Come, ye children, hearken unto me: I will teach you the fear of the Lord. What man is he that desireth life, and loveth many days, that he may see good? Keep thy tongue from evil, and thy lips from speaking guile. Depart from evil, and do good; seek peace, and pursue it. The eyes of the Lord are upon the righteous, and his ears are open unto their cry. The face of the Lord is against them that do evil, to cut off the remembrance of them from the earth. The righteous cry, and the Lord heareth, and delivereth them out of all their troubles. The Lord is nigh unto them that are of a broken heart; and saveth such as be of a contrite spirit. Many are the afflictions of the righteous: but the Lord delivereth him out of them all. He keepeth all his bones: not one of them is broken. Evil shall slay the wicked: and they that hate the righteous shall be desolate. The Lord redeemeth the soul of his servants: and none of them that trust in him shall be desolate.

Psalm 55

My mother experienced God's victory over evildoers countless times in her life, which is why she loved this psalm.

Give ear to my prayer, O God; and hide not thyself from my supplication. Attend unto me, and hear me: I mourn in my complaint, and make a noise; Because of the voice of the enemy, because of the oppression of the wicked: for they cast iniquity upon me, and in wrath they hate me. My heart is sore pained within me: and the terrors of death are fallen upon me. Fearfulness and trembling are come upon me, and horror hath overwhelmed me. And I said, Oh that I had wings like a dove! for then would I fly away, and be at rest. Lo, then would I wander far off, and remain in the wilderness. Selah.

I would hasten my escape from the windy storm and tempest. Destroy, O Lord, and divide their tongues: for I have seen violence and strife in the city. Day and night they go about it upon the walls thereof: mischief also and sorrow are in the midst of it. Wickedness is in the midst thereof: deceit and guile depart not from her streets. For it was not an enemy that reproached me; then I could have borne it: neither was it he that hated me that did magnify himself against me; then I would have hid myself from him: But it was thou, a man mine equal, my guide, and mine acquaintance. We took sweet counsel together, and walked unto the house of God in company. Let death seize upon them, and let them go down quick into hell: for wickedness is in their dwellings, and among them. As for me, I will call upon God; and the Lord shall save me. Evening, and morning, and at noon, will I pray, and cry aloud: and he shall hear my voice. He hath delivered my soul in peace from the battle that was against me: for there were many with me. God shall hear, and afflict them, even he that abideth of old. Selah. Because they have no changes, therefore they fear not God. He hath put forth his hands against such as be at peace with him: he hath broken his covenant. The words of his mouth were smoother than butter, but war was in his heart: his words were softer than oil, yet were they drawn swords. Cast thy burden upon the Lord, and he shall sustain thee: he shall never suffer the righteous to be moved. But thou, O God, shalt bring them down into the pit of destruction: bloody and deceitful men shall not live out half their days; but I will trust in thee.

Isaiah 41:13

One of my mother's favorite verses. This was the source of her tremendous courage.

For I the LORD thy God will hold thy right hand, saying unto thee, Fear not; I will help thee.

Isaiah 41:10

Despite how working as a tailor negatively affected her health, my mother trusted God throughout her entire life and never felt let down by Him.

Fear thou not; for I am with thee: be not dismayed; for I am thy God: I will strengthen thee; yea, I will help thee; yea, I will uphold thee with the right hand of my righteousness.

John 10:1-10

Everything that happens in our lives leads us to an awareness that God wants nothing more than abundance for us in every aspect of lives.

Verily, verily, I say unto you, He that entereth not by the door into the sheepfold, but climbeth up some other way, the same is a thief and a robber. But he that entereth in by the door is the shepherd of the sheep. To him the porter openeth; and the sheep hear his voice: and he calleth his own sheep by name, and leadeth them out. And when he putteth forth his own sheep, he goeth before them, and the sheep follow him: for they know his voice. And a stranger will they not follow, but will flee from him: for they know not the voice of strangers. This parable spake Jesus unto them: but they understood not what things they were which he spake unto them. Then said Jesus unto them again, Verily, verily, I say unto you, I am the door of the sheep. All that ever came before me are thieves and robbers: but the sheep did not hear them. I am the door: by me if any man enter in, he shall be saved, and shall go in and out, and find pasture. The thief cometh not, but for to steal, and to kill, and to destroy: I am come that they might have life, and that they might have it more abundantly.

Christine Lee, The Educator

Christine Lee is an educator and owner of Yuin University. A self-starting entrepreneur, her vision is to help students become adaptable beings by immersing them in a teaching experience that is safe, secure and financially viable. With this mission in mind, it is her vision to help her students and colleagues alike, hone in on a paradigm shift, within the system to foster more lucrative and collaborative working environments to secure their future.

For more information on Yuin University please visit our website: www.yuin.edu

Connect with Christine Lee, The Author

She definitely believes that we all have a story inside us. A mentee of Bob Proctor and an affiliate of the PGI (Proctor Gallagher Institute), Christine would love to connect with you and give you some personal insights into her voyage into becoming an author, educator and business woman. Connect directly with Christine by email: inyekim@gmail.com or christine@yuin.edu

For more information on Bob Proctor and PGI, connect via their website here: https://www.proctorgallagher.institute/programs/bob-proctor-coaching/

Another Side of Christine...

Energy is essential for all of us to sustain a healthy balanced life and this has been paramount for Christine's successful endeavors. She is the owner of an acupuncture clinic, which focuses on the ancient art of healing through activating pressure points to help with the flow in one's body. The most important flow is our *chi*, which is what makes up the sum of our energy. With dwindling energy, it is very difficult to accomplish simple daily tasks. At the Yuin Acupuncture Centre, Christine prides herself in introducing her audience to an ancient Asian cultural wisdom, so they can immerse themselves into a session while learning to feel more vibrant. For more information on this traditional art of energy flow please visit: https://www.facebook.com/yuinacupunctureclinic

For a limited time only, the clinic is offering a discount on their services for anyone who purchases the book. Email Christine with this promo code: #getyourchiback2021, with proof of purchase for "My Hero- A Love Letter to my Mother" and retrieve your DISCOUNTED offer.

Connect on Social Media

LinkedIn: https://www.linkedin.com/in/christinelee2011/
Facebook: https://www.facebook.com/ChrLee12
Instagram: chrlee122018

Christine's mission is to show the world that she has multi layers to her brand, which will be highlighted with some upcoming information through her website and social media handles. Follow this author on social media for future updates.

"My Hero- A Love Letter to my Mother" is available on Amazon.

ABOUT THE AUTHOR

Christine is an entrepreneur, real estate agent and a chair at Yuin University in Southern California. She lives in the United States with her family.

Christine has led a very colorful life and relies heavily on legacy, culture and history to assist her in her thought process. A third culture woman from Korea, Christine moved to the United States when she was a child. The deep parts of her roots and upbringing has led her to many different parts of the world.

As a mentee of Bob Proctor's teachings, Christine follows a very simple law, which is the law of attraction. Her success has been guided by Bob's masterful teachings and has opened up a pathway for her to write her debut book, *My Hero. – A Love Letter to my Mother.* Her life was transformed when she registered for one of Bob's monumental events in LA entitled the "Science of Getting". Mesmerized by the experience, Christine embarked on a journey to invest in herself to become part of his elite circle. Since 2014, Christine has put Bob's teaching at the forefront of her mind to create a life of abundance and success. He visited her school campus during that year and inspired her colleagues and students on practices geared towards a life full of prosperity, abundance and serenity.

In her book, Christine reflects on how her mother is her eternal hero, and with that in mind, she would like to inspire people to look toward their parents as a solid foundation for their own paradigms; good or bad. It is in this book, that Christine found a way to celebrate her family and immaculate traditional values which is connected to all of the work she does. She is a true believer that investing and reinvesting in yourself, is the perfect way to make connections with people. When she studies herself, she is more open to living her life by design.

Giving a Voice to Creativity!

With every donation, a voice will be given to
the creativity that lies within the hearts of
our children living with diverse challenges.

By making this difference, children that may
not have been given the opportunity to have their
Heart Heard will have the freedom to create
beautiful works of art and musical creations.

Donate by visiting

HeartstobeHeard.com

We thank you.

Made in the USA
Las Vegas, NV
27 January 2021